Creative Writing Space

I0435951

The Time Is Always Write Now!

Creative Writing Space Workbook

Alicia "WATERS"

THE TIME IS ALWAYS WRITE NOW!

Creative Writing Space

www.anwempires@gmail.com

ISBN:13:978-1505663921

Printed in the United States of America by Create Space

Designing Your Sacred Writing Space

THE TIME IS ALWAYS WRITE NOW!

Creative Writing Space

The Time Is Always Write Now, is designed to be a creative writing space workbook for recording ideas, writing drafts and so much more. Though, writing might come naturally to some, for others the grove of writing can seem like a chore. However, no matter whether you are an avid writer or not, it is always time to write even if it is the simplest idea or having brainstorming moments for flushing out our thoughts.

This workbook is designed to create a sacred space for your writings of all sorts. This workbook can also function as a tablet to keep all of your writings organized in one space. The goal is to record your brilliance and design your personal authentic writing journey within these pages.

Create your best writing creations yet, plan your blog posts and/or draw images that randomly come into your mind. No matter what type of writing that you choose to do, just write. There is always something to write about including gratitude moments. Again, your choice of writing is entirely up to you, the goal is to just write something as often as possible.

The time is now to bring forth what is inside of you to grace the world with your gifts or just for you to reflect on your own personal writing evolution. So, go ahead and freely express yourself on the pages of the creative writing space. Your Time Is "Write" Now!

THE TIME IS ALWAYS WRITE NOW!

The Time Is Always Write Now!

Creative Writing Space Section

Creative Writing Space

THE TIME IS ALWAYS WRITE NOW!

Creative Writing Space

THE TIME IS ALWAYS WRITE NOW!

Creative Writing Space

THE TIME IS ALWAYS WRITE NOW!

Creative Writing Space

THE TIME IS ALWAYS WRITE NOW!

Creative Writing Space

THE TIME IS ALWAYS WRITE NOW!

Creative Writing Space

THE TIME IS ALWAYS WRITE NOW!

Creative Writing Space

THE TIME IS ALWAYS WRITE NOW!

Creative Writing Space

THE TIME IS ALWAYS WRITE NOW!

Creative Writing Space

THE TIME IS ALWAYS WRITE NOW!

Creative Writing Space

THE TIME IS ALWAYS WRITE NOW!

Creative Writing Space

THE TIME IS ALWAYS WRITE NOW!

Creative Writing Space

THE TIME IS ALWAYS WRITE NOW!

Creative Writing Space

THE TIME IS ALWAYS WRITE NOW!

Creative Writing Space

THE TIME IS ALWAYS WRITE NOW!

Creative Writing Space

THE TIME IS ALWAYS WRITE NOW!

Creative Writing Space

THE TIME IS ALWAYS WRITE NOW!

Creative Writing Space

THE TIME IS ALWAYS WRITE NOW!

Creative Writing Space

THE TIME IS ALWAYS WRITE NOW!

Creative Writing Space

THE TIME IS ALWAYS WRITE NOW!

Creative Writing Space

THE TIME IS ALWAYS WRITE NOW!

Creative Writing Space

THE TIME IS ALWAYS WRITE NOW!

Creative Writing Space

THE TIME IS ALWAYS WRITE NOW!

Creative Writing Space

Creative Writing Space

THE TIME IS ALWAYS WRITE NOW!

Creative Writing Space

THE TIME IS ALWAYS WRITE NOW!

Creative Writing Space

THE TIME IS ALWAYS WRITE NOW!

Creative Writing Space

THE TIME IS ALWAYS WRITE NOW!

Creative Writing Space

THE TIME IS ALWAYS WRITE NOW!

Creative Writing Space

THE TIME IS ALWAYS WRITE NOW!

Creative Writing Space

THE TIME IS ALWAYS WRITE NOW!

Creative Writing Space

THE TIME IS ALWAYS WRITE NOW!

Creative Writing Space

THE TIME IS ALWAYS WRITE NOW!

Creative Writing Space

THE TIME IS ALWAYS WRITE NOW!

Creative Writing Space

THE TIME IS ALWAYS WRITE NOW!

Creative Writing Space

THE TIME IS ALWAYS WRITE NOW!

Creative Writing Space

THE TIME IS ALWAYS WRITE NOW!

Creative Writing Space

THE TIME IS ALWAYS WRITE NOW!

Creative Writing Space

THE TIME IS ALWAYS WRITE NOW!

Creative Writing Space

THE TIME IS ALWAYS WRITE NOW!

Creative Writing Space

THE TIME IS ALWAYS WRITE NOW!

Creative Writing Space

THE TIME IS ALWAYS WRITE NOW!

Creative Writing Space

THE TIME IS ALWAYS WRITE NOW!

Creative Writing Space

THE TIME IS ALWAYS WRITE NOW!

Creative Writing Space

THE TIME IS ALWAYS WRITE NOW!

Creative Writing Space

THE TIME IS ALWAYS WRITE NOW!

Creative Writing Space

THE TIME IS ALWAYS WRITE NOW!

Creative Writing Space

THE TIME IS ALWAYS WRITE NOW!

Creative Writing Space

THE TIME IS ALWAYS WRITE NOW!

Creative Writing Space

THE TIME IS ALWAYS WRITE NOW!

Creative Writing Space

THE TIME IS ALWAYS WRITE NOW!

Creative Writing Space

THE TIME IS ALWAYS WRITE NOW!

Creative Writing Space

THE TIME IS ALWAYS WRITE NOW!

Creative Writing Space

THE TIME IS ALWAYS WRITE NOW!

Creative Writing Space

THE TIME IS ALWAYS WRITE NOW!

Creative Writing Space

THE TIME IS ALWAYS WRITE NOW!

Creative Writing Space

THE TIME IS ALWAYS WRITE NOW!

Creative Writing Space

THE TIME IS ALWAYS WRITE NOW!

Creative Writing Space

THE TIME IS ALWAYS WRITE NOW!

Creative Writing Space

THE TIME IS ALWAYS WRITE NOW!

Creative Writing Space

THE TIME IS ALWAYS WRITE NOW!

Creative Writing Space

THE TIME IS ALWAYS WRITE NOW!

Creative Writing Space

THE TIME IS ALWAYS WRITE NOW!

Creative Writing Space

THE TIME IS ALWAYS WRITE NOW!

Creative Writing Space

THE TIME IS ALWAYS WRITE NOW!

Creative Writing Space

THE TIME IS ALWAYS WRITE NOW!

Creative Writing Space

THE TIME IS ALWAYS WRITE NOW!

Creative Writing Space

THE TIME IS ALWAYS WRITE NOW!

Creative Writing Space

THE TIME IS ALWAYS WRITE NOW!

Creative Writing Space

THE TIME IS ALWAYS WRITE NOW!

Creative Writing Space

THE TIME IS ALWAYS WRITE NOW!

Creative Writing Space

THE TIME IS ALWAYS WRITE NOW!

Creative Writing Space

THE TIME IS ALWAYS WRITE NOW!

Creative Writing Space

THE TIME IS ALWAYS WRITE NOW!

Creative Writing Space

THE TIME IS ALWAYS WRITE NOW!

Creative Writing Space

THE TIME IS ALWAYS WRITE NOW!

Creative Writing Space

THE TIME IS ALWAYS WRITE NOW!

Creative Writing Space

THE TIME IS ALWAYS WRITE NOW!

Creative Writing Space

THE TIME IS ALWAYS WRITE NOW!

Creative Writing Space

THE TIME IS ALWAYS WRITE NOW!

Creative Writing Space

THE TIME IS ALWAYS WRITE NOW!

Creative Writing Space

THE TIME IS ALWAYS WRITE NOW!

Creative Writing Space

THE TIME IS ALWAYS WRITE NOW!

Creative Writing Space

For More Resources

Visit:

www.getitdonewritenow.blogspot.com

www.amazon.com/author/alicianwaters

Or

To Book the Author

For Speaking Engagements

Email: www.anwempires@gmail.com

If you enjoyed this resource, please consider writing a review on Amazon.com

Thanks & Blessings!

THE TIME IS ALWAYS WRITE NOW!

Abstract

The Automated Biometric Identification System (IDENT) is the central DHS-wide system for storage and processing of biometric and associated biographic information for national security; law enforcement; immigration and border management; intelligence; background investigations for national security positions and certain positions of public trust; and associated testing, training, management reporting, planning and analysis, or other administrative uses. This Privacy Impact Assessment (PIA) and the attached appendices provide transparency into how the system uses personally identifiable information (PII) and details the system's sharing partners and functions. As such, the IDENT PIAs of July 31, 2006, and May 25, 2007; the US-VISIT/DHS and United Kingdom Border Agency's (UKBA) International Group Visa Services Project PIA of July 2, 2008; and the Five Country Conference (FCC) PIA of November 2, 2009, will be retired upon publication of this PIA.

Overview

The legacy Immigration and Naturalization Service (INS) developed IDENT in 1994 as a law enforcement system for collecting and processing biometrics. In 2004, the Department of Homeland Security (DHS) established the U.S. Visitor and Immigrant Status Indicator Technology (US-VISIT) Program as the first large-scale biometric identification program to support immigration and border management. IDENT has evolved over the years into the central DHS-wide system for the storage and processing of biometric data. IDENT stores and processes biometric data—digital fingerprints, photographs, iris scans, and facial images—and links biometrics with biographic information to establish and verify identities. IDENT serves as a biographic and biometric repository for the Department. As a data steward, US-VISIT provides a service to its data providers and data users. US-VISIT identifies each collection by data provider and its authority to use, retain, and share it. IDENT enables sharing with authorized users after the data provider has approved the sharing.

The process of retaining data provided to IDENT is referred to as *enrollment*. Each time an individual's biometrics are enrolled in IDENT, it is an *encounter*. Adding encounters to an already existing identity is referred to as an *assignment*. With each encounter, IDENT:

- Checks a person's biometrics against the IDENT watchlist of known or suspected terrorists (KST), criminals, and immigration violators;
- Checks a person's biometrics against the entire database of fingerprints to help determine if a person is using an alias and/or attempting to use fraudulent identification; and
- Checks a person's biometrics against those associated with the identification document presented to help ensure that the document belongs to the person presenting it and not someone else.

IDENT automatically compares the biometrics from each new encounter to the best quality biometrics associated with each identity in the system. IDENT assigns a new identity for the encounter if an encounter does not match an identity already in the system. If the new encounter matches an identity in the system, then IDENT appends the encounter to the existing encounters for that identity. IDENT processes are governed by IDENT's data users and data providers. US-VISIT provides different levels of

Privacy Impact Assessment
for the

Automated Biometric Identification System (IDENT)

DHS/NPPD/USVISIT/PIA-002

December 7, 2012

access and services to both IDENT data users and data providers based on the purpose of the initial biometric collection and subsequent sharing and retention.

IDENT Users

IDENT users are entities that query IDENT and may also use IDENT to upload and store biometric information. All IDENT users are federal, state, local, tribal, foreign, or international governmental agencies that have entered into written information sharing access agreements (e.g., memoranda of understanding (MOU)) with US-VISIT for biometric identification and analysis services.[1] An IDENT user that does not store biometric information has "search only" access, meaning they can search IDENT in order to accurately identify domestic and international threats through subject-of-interest queries. These queries allow IDENT users to search IDENT using their own data, but that data is not enrolled (or maintained) in IDENT. Depending on the agreement with DHS, the IDENT user may search only the IDENT watchlist or the entire IDENT gallery.

IDENT Data Providers

Not all IDENT users provide their data for retention in IDENT. The subset of IDENT users that contribute and store data to IDENT are referred to as IDENT data providers.[2] IDENT data providers may contribute data to IDENT in two ways:

- *Search and Enroll:* The data provider provides data to conduct an IDENT search and enrolls that data as a new IDENT encounter.

- *Search and Assign:* The data provider provides data to conduct an IDENT search, which enrolls as a new IDENT encounter only if another encounter already exists. These data providers cannot create a new identity in IDENT; they can only add encounters to an already existing identity.

Data providers determine the IDENT users that their data can be shared with based on data provider rules and approved DHS mission needs.

IDENT users include:

U.S. Customs and Border Protection (CBP): CBP searches and enrolls data in IDENT. CBP enrolls data in IDENT to screen all in-scope international travelers[3] to the United States, persons

---

[1] DHS components are not required to enter into MOUs with US-VISIT.

[2] In very limited circumstances, a provider may only store data and does not receive a response. For example, the Department of Defense may provide data via CD to be included in the IDENT data repository, but receives no response.

[3] In-scope international travelers excludes:
- U.S. citizens;
- Canadian citizens visiting the United States temporarily for business or pleasure who are not otherwise required to present a visa or be issued Form I-94 or Form I-95 for admission or parole into the United States;
- Visitors admitted on an A-1, A-2, C-3, G-1, G-2, G-3, G-4, NATO-1, NATO-2, NATO-3, NATO-4, NATO-5, or NATO-6 visa;
- Children under the age of 14 (unless participating in a trusted traveler program);
- Persons over the age of 79;

using a trusted traveler program,[4] and anyone interdicted while crossing the border illegally. As part of the screening process, CBP officers collect digital fingerprints and a digital photograph from all in-scope, non-U.S. citizen travelers and those travelers approved for enrollment in a CBP trusted traveler program. Trusted traveler programs allow CBP to expedite the inspection and security process for lower risk travelers and apply more scrutiny to travelers who present higher risks to the United States. Using US-VISIT's IDENT, CBP officers may also quickly verify whether an individual applying for entry to the United States is the same individual to whom a visa was issued based on the biometrics provided through the visa process.

- Immigration and Customs Enforcement (ICE): ICE searches and enrolls data in IDENT. ICE uses IDENT to enroll biometrics about individuals encountered and/or arrested for criminal or immigration violations through the course of an investigation, arrest, booking, detention, and/or removal from the United States. ICE also compares those individuals' biometrics against IDENT to find or verify identity, or to identify threats. Additionally, ICE uses IDENT data as well as data from other sources to identify individuals who may have overstayed the terms of their admission.[5]

- U.S. Coast Guard (USCG): USCG searches and enrolls data in IDENT to assist in the apprehension and prosecution of illegal migrants and migrant smugglers at sea. USCG uses mobile biometric collection devices—handheld scanners and cameras—to collect and compare migrants' biometric information against information about criminals and immigration violators.[6] USCG also uses IDENT to pre-vet and then verify crew aboard High Interest Vessels.

- U.S. Citizenship and Immigration Services (USCIS): USCIS searches and enrolls data in IDENT to establish and verify the identities of individuals applying for immigration benefits, including asylum and refugee status.[7]

- Department of State (DoS): DoS searches and enrolls data in IDENT and uses IDENT to establish and verify the identities of visa applicants at embassies and consulates around the world through its BioVisa program. Consular officers also use this information in determining visa eligibility. DoS Office of Personnel Security and Suitability (OPSS) also uses IDENT for personnel security and suitability determinations.[8]

- Classes of visitors the Secretary of State and the Secretary of Homeland Security jointly determine shall be exempt;
- An individual visitor the Secretary of State and the Secretary of Homeland Security or the Director of Central Intelligence Agency jointly determine shall be exempt; and
- Taiwanese officials who hold E-1 visas and members of their immediate families who hold E-1 visas.

[4] See DHS/CBP/PIA-002(a) – Global Enrollment System Update, http://www.dhs.gov/xlibrary/assets/privacy/privacy_pia_cbp_goes.pdf
[5] See DHS/ALL/PIA-041 – One DHS Overstay Vetting Pilot PIA, http://www.dhs.gov/files/publications/gc_1282922720391.shtm#40.
[6] See DHS/USCG/PIA-002(c) - United States Coast Guard "Biometrics at Sea" PIA, http://www.dhs.gov/files/publications/gc_1281126129297.shtm#1.
[7] See DHS/USCIS/PIA-033 - Immigration Benefits Background Check Systems PIA, http://www.dhs.gov/files/publications/gc_1279308495679.shtm#33.
[8] OPSS sharing is discussed in full in the US-VISIT DHS-DOJ Interoperability PIA, appendix B found at www.dhs.gov/privacy.

- Department of Defense (DOD) and the Intelligence Community: DOD searches and enrolls data in IDENT. US-VISIT works across the federal Intelligence Community and DOD to promote intelligence efforts in identifying persons who may be a threat to the United States. DOD collects information to support its military mission, detainee affairs, and force protection efforts; as well as its antiterrorism, special operations, stability operations, homeland defense, counterintelligence, and intelligence efforts around the world. Additionally, DOD enrolls information collected from non-U.S. citizens denied access to military posts. This information may be shared with US-VISIT biometric services to facilitate identification of terrorists. Finally, DOD enrolls data in IDENT to help identify KSTs by matching against known and latent fingerprints collected from terrorist safe houses and ongoing criminal investigations.

- Department of Justice (DOJ) and state and local law enforcement: DOJ and state and local law enforcement search IDENT to ensure they have accurate identity information about individuals they encounter. US-VISIT is improving integration, accessibility, and interoperability with other law enforcement and intelligence systems. DHS and the Federal Bureau of Investigation (FBI) have established interoperability between IDENT and the FBI's Integrated Automated Fingerprint Identification System (IAFIS) fingerprint databases. DHS has published and is updating a separate DHS-DOJ Interoperability PIA detailing IDENT-IAFIS Interoperability. Interoperability enables sharing of biometric and related biographic, criminal history, and immigration information to meet the respective agencies' missions.

- Federal, state, and local investigative agencies: The investigative agencies search and enroll data in IDENT. This data is useful to the DHS mission in identifying national security threats, or inadmissible aliens. US-VISIT's Biometric Support Center (BSC), staffed by highly-trained fingerprint examiners, verifies biometrics to help identify John or Jane Does, and support terrorist investigations.

- Foreign partners: Foreign government law enforcement, intelligence, and criminal agencies, as well as international entities (such as the International Criminal Police Organization (INTERPOL)) search and enroll biometric data with DHS. Information collected by foreign partners that is shared with U.S. law enforcement and immigration officials and protected by U.S. laws, international agreements, and additional implementation agreements and established protocols.

IDENT Data Elements

Data can be transmitted from IDENT to internal and external systems on a real-time basis, on a regularized and manual basis, and can be transmitted on a single or periodic *ad hoc* basis.

IDENT records contain variations of data depending on the type of encounter. Depending on the information sharing agreement, data users will receive different amounts of information back. A record stored in IDENT may contain the following data elements:[9]

---

[9] An IDENT user or data provider may receive all available data elements listed. This is also known as a full IDENT response.

Biometric data: digital facial photographs, fingerprints, iris scans, palm prints, latent fingerprints[10] (collected by federal, state, local, and foreign law enforcement agencies, and military operations for an investigation or for intelligence purposes), and other biometric modalities to be added in the future.

Biographic data: (1) full name (i.e., first, middle, last, nicknames, and aliases), date of birth (DOB), gender, signature; personal identifiers including Alien Registration Number (A-number), Social Security number (SSN) (when provided), state identification number, civil record number, Federal Bureau of Investigation (FBI) Fingerprint Number (FNU), Fingerprint Identification Number (FIN), National Unique Identification Number (NUIN); and personal physical details, such as height, weight, eye color, and hair color; (2) identifiers for citizenship and nationality, including person-centric details, such as country of birth, country of citizenship, and nationality; (3) derogatory information (DI),[11] if applicable, including wants and warrants, KSTs, sexual offender registration, and immigration violations; (4) IDENT watchlist status information; (5) miscellaneous officer comment information; (6) document information and identifiers (e.g., passport and visa data; document type; document number; and country of issuance); and (7) current and historic whereabouts.

Encounter data: transaction identifier data, such as sending organization; timestamp; workstation; reason fingerprinted, such as entry, visa application, credentialing application, or apprehension; and any available encounter information, including an IDENT-generated encounter identification number (EID).

Test and training data: biometric data that may be real or simulated, and biographic and encounter-related data for use only by US-VISIT personnel for testing and training purposes.

IDENT Watchlist

The IDENT watchlist provides a repository of biometric information on persons of interest, including wants and warrants from federal, state, local, tribal, and international law enforcement agencies through the FBI; KSTs; deported felons and absconders, sexual offender registrants, gang-related records, subjects who have violated U.S. immigration laws or who have been denied a biometric visa (BioVisa) by DoS; and other persons of interest to DHS. US-VISIT data providers, as well as selected US-VISIT staff (such as those assigned to the visa overstay program) provide the data and indicate whether the particular individual should appear in the IDENT watchlist in accordance with standard operating procedures, which include reviews of provided data and confirmation that the data meets established watchlist criteria. IDENT users do not use the IDENT watchlist to make a final determination, but instead use the watchlist to flag individuals who may be of interest to individual US-VISIT users. Further analysis is conducted by the IDENT users upon a match in IDENT pursuant to their specific programmatic authorities.

IDENT Data Sharing

Through IDENT, US-VISIT provides the results of biometric checks to authorized users, to help

---

[10] Fingerprints that are present but not retrieved directly from the individual/subject (e.g., prints pulled from a crime scene) and lack identification.

[11] A set of data related to negative or criminal information associated with an encounter.

them accurately identify individuals they encounter pursuant to their missions and determine whether those individuals pose possible threats to the United States. The users' responses may include some or all the information from an individual's previous IDENT encounters.

In addition to sharing previous encounters, IDENT may allow data providers to receive notifications of subsequent IDENT encounters for a specific individual. This notification function is referred to as wrap-back.[12] The data provider must enroll data on the specific individual in order to receive wrap-back notifications on that individual. IDENT users that do not enroll data on an individual may not subscribe to wrap-back data for that individual.

IDENT does not share all encounter data with every user. Although US-VISIT is the steward of the data, each data provider is able to restrict the maintenance, retention, and sharing of its data with other organizations. For example, organization-level data filtering is applied to asylum data so that only approved organizations can access that data.

All authorized IDENT users can query IDENT to receive a simple yes/no response. In cases where there is a positive response, the IDENT user will need to contact US-VISIT for additional information about the hit. This also holds true in cases of a confirmed match of a latent print in IDENT; the submitting agency can request additional information on the individual.

Privacy Risks and Mitigations

US-VISIT has identified several general privacy risks associated with the IDENT system and data sharing activities. The first risk is that individuals may not know their data is enrolled into IDENT. This risk is mitigated by the fact that in most instances, information is collected directly from the individual, so the individual knows his or her fingerprints are being captured at the time of collection. US-VISIT also mitigates this risk through publication of this PIA. In addition, IDENT data providers may provide notice through publication of their own PIAs and other methods.

Secondly, there is a privacy risk that an individual's biometrics may be matched with the wrong biographics. US-VISIT mitigates this risk through three processes: manual fingerprint comparisons, fingerprint quality checks by the data provider, and the transition from 2-print matching to 10-print matching. The National Institute of Standards and Technology (NIST) advocates collecting more fingerprints to improve the accuracy of identifying individuals.[13] Additionally, US-VISIT provides a redress process for individuals who believe the data held on them in IDENT is inaccurate. Section 2.4 discusses these processes at length.

---

[12] Wrap-back functionality allows data providers to specify events or a condition for automatic notification when a subject meets a pre-established system parameter, such as if a subject reaches a particular watchlist level. The data provider must enroll their data as "search and enroll" to receive wrap-back.

[13] *See* Testimony of Dr. Martin Herman, Chief, Information Access Division, Information Technology Laboratory, National Institute of Standards and Technology before the U.S. House of Representatives Committee on Homeland Security, Subcommittee on Economic Security, Infrastructure Protection, and Cybersecurity, *Ensuring the Security of America's Borders through the Use of Biometric Passports and other Identity Documents* (June 22, 2005). http://www.nist.gov/testimony/2005/mherman_house_hs_biometrics_6-22.html.

A third privacy risk is the retention of data longer than needed. DHS is re-evaluating the existing retention policy to determine whether a new retention period or combination of retention periods is appropriate. DHS will publish a PIA update for any change in the retention period.

Another privacy risk inherent to IDENT as a system with many sharing partners is the risk that data are shared with IDENT users or data providers who do not have appropriate authority or a need to know the specific data. For example, IDENT data collected via CBP's Trusted Traveler program may be shared in limited circumstances, but will not be accessed by local law enforcement officials in the course of a routine traffic stop. The risk of this data being inappropriately shared is mitigated by US-VISIT's Data Access Security Controls. US-VISIT restricts the maintenance and sharing of IDENT data with users through Data Access Security Controls; these controls allow owning organizations to control what data is shared and who is granted access to that data. The restrictions are formalized by written data sharing agreements with sharing partners. US-VISIT is able to enforce these written agreements through audits for appropriate use after the agreement is in place. In some cases, an additional access control exists requiring the user conducting the query to contact US-VISIT before information will be released.

Related to the risk of sharing is the separate risk of sharing IDENT data with foreign partners, where it is more difficult for DHS to externally impose the same controls that govern the data internally. These risks are mitigated by those foreign partners' audit and redress provisions, which are identified in the process of negotiating a data sharing agreement. This PIA lends additional transparency to those external partners' provisions by outlining them in appendices to this PIA.

Finally, there is a risk of information about special, legally protected classes of individuals being shared inappropriately. IDENT contains information related to aliens who receive special legal protections generally prohibiting disclosure to anyone beyond DHS, DOJ, and DoS, unless the disclosure fits within certain delineated exceptions (e.g., to a law enforcement official for a legitimate law enforcement purpose). US-VISIT is currently developing the technological means to filter these classes of individuals' data from access by certain data users. In the meantime, US-VISIT is restricting certain users' access to the protected information.

This PIA explains access and handling by DHS IDENT users. The appendices to the PIA explain access and handling by external users, users outside of DHS.

Section 1.0 Authorities and Other Requirements

1.1 What specific legal authorities and/or agreements permit and define the collection of information by the project in question?

The data in IDENT is collected, processed, and stored consistent with the applicable authorities of the agencies and programs that originally collected the data. These authorities are described in the PIAs, System of Records Notice (SORN), or other materials for each of these programs. IDENT serves as a biographic and biometric repository for the Department. As a data steward, US-VISIT provides a service to its data providers and data users. US-VISIT identifies each collection by data provider and its authority to use, retain, and share it. IDENT enables sharing with authorized users after the data provider has approved the sharing.

The statutory and other authorities pertaining to the establishment and mission of the US-VISIT program, including the operation and maintenance of IDENT, include:

- Section 2(a) of the Immigration and Naturalization Service Data Management Improvement Act of 2000, Public Law 106–215, 114 Stat. 337 (June 15, 2000);
- Section 110 of the Illegal Immigration Reform and Immigrant Responsibility Act of 1996, Public Law No. 104-208, Div. C, 110 Stat. 3009-546 (Sept. 30, 1996);
- Section 205 of the Visa Waiver Permanent Program Act of 2000, Public Law 106–396, 114 Stat. 1637, 1641 (October 30, 2000);
- Sections 403(c) and 414(b) of the Uniting and Strengthening America by Providing Appropriate Tools Required to Intercept and Obstruct Terrorism Act of 2001 (USA PATRIOT ACT) , Public Law 107–56, 115 Stat. 272, 344, 353 (October 26, 2001);
- Section 302 of the Enhanced Border Security and Visa Entry Reform Act of 2002, Public Law 107–173, 116 Stat. 543, 552 (May 14, 2002);
- Section 7208 of the Intelligence Reform and Terrorism Prevention Act of 2004, Public Law 108-458, 118 Stat. 3638, 3817 (December 17, 2004);
- Section 711 of the Implementing Recommendations of the 9/11 Commission Act of 2007, Public Law 110-53, 121 Stat. 266, 338 (August 3, 2007);
- 8 CFR § 214.1, Department of Homeland Security, Immigration Regulations, Nonimmigrant Classes, Requirements for Admission, extension and maintenance of status (January 1, 2012).
- 8 CFR § 235.1, Department of Homeland Security, Immigration Regulations, Inspection of Persons Applying for Admission, Scope of Examination (January 1, 2012).
- Homeland Security Presidential Directive/HSPD-11: Comprehensive Terrorist Related Procedures (August 27, 2004); and
- Homeland Security Presidential Directive/HSPD-24: Biometrics for Identification and Screening to Enhance National Security (June 5, 2008).

Agencies may collect Social Security Numbers (SSN) either as a required data field or when an applicant provides the information at a Port of Entry (POE) pursuant to the Data Provider's specific authority.

1.2   What Privacy Act System of Records Notice(s) (SORN(s)) apply to the information?

The information in IDENT is covered by the DHS/NPPD/US-VISIT-0004 - IDENT SORN, 72 Fed. Reg. 31080 (Jun. 5, 2007). This SORN is currently being revised and will be re-published.

1.3   Has a system security plan been completed for the information system(s) supporting the project?

IDENT received a 3-year authority to operate (ATO) on May 4, 2010.

US-VISIT has completed a System Security Plan (SSP) for the IDENT system. The IDENT SSP, dated April 30, 2010, complies with the NIST Special Publication (SP) Recommended Security Controls for Federal Information Systems (NIST SP 800-53) and the DHS National Security Sensitive Systems Handbook and Policy Directive 4300 A, version 5.5.

1.4 Does a records retention schedule approved by the National Archives and Records Administration (NARA) exist?

The National Archives and Records Administration (NARA) approved the records retention schedule for the IDENT system. The records schedule requires US-VISIT to maintain IDENT records in its custody for 75 years or when no longer needed for legal or business purposes, whichever is later (N1-563-08-34). DHS is re-evaluating the current retention policy to determine whether a new retention period or combination of retention periods is appropriate. DHS will publish a PIA update for any change in the retention period.

1.5 If the information is covered by the Paperwork Reduction Act (PRA), provide the OMB Control number and the agency number for the collection. If there are multiple forms, include a list in an appendix.

DHS requires certain aliens who cross the borders of the United States to provide fingerprints, photographs, and/or other biometric identifiers upon their arrival and departure at designated ports. These requirements constitute an information collection under the Paperwork Reduction Act (PRA), 44 U.S.C. § 4501, *et seq*. The Office of Management and Budget (OMB), in accordance with the PRA, has previously approved this information collection. The OMB Control Number for this collection is 1600-0006. The US-VISIT PRA Notice covers US-VISIT collection activities covered by the regulatory notice of the program. There are no forms associated with this collection because the information is collected electronically. All other information stored in US-VISIT systems is collected by IDENT data providers and stored under the data provider agency's regulatory notices and authorities. The data that is stored in IDENT supports the DHS mission.

Section 2.0 Characterization of the Information

The following questions are intended to define the scope of the information requested and/or collected, as well as reasons for its collection.

2.1 Identify the information the project collects, uses, disseminates, or maintains.

The types of data stored in IDENT include biometric, biographic, and encounter-related information for the operational, production, testing, and training environments of US-VISIT to support national security, law enforcement, criminal justice, immigration and border management, and intelligence purposes; to conduct background investigations for national security positions and certain positions of public trust; and to provide associated testing, training, management reporting, planning and analysis, or other administrative uses. IDENT receives biometric and associated biographic data from DHS and external users. DHS and external users then conduct biometric searches against IDENT. At the request of or with the permission of a user, IDENT may store biometric and associated biographic data to support the DHS mission, such as:

Biometric data: digital facial photographs, fingerprints, iris scans, palm prints, latent fingerprints (collected by federal, state, local, and foreign law enforcement agencies, or military operations for an investigation or for intelligence purposes).

Biographic data: 1) full name (i.e., first, middle, last, nicknames, and aliases), date of birth, gender, signature, personal identifiers, including but not limited to Alien Registration Number, Social Security number (when provided), state identification number, civil record number, Federal Bureau of Investigation Fingerprint Number, Fingerprint Identification Number, National Unique Identification Number, and personal physical details, such as height, weight, eye color, and hair color; 2) identifiers for citizenship and nationality, including person-centric details, such as country of birth, country of citizenship, and nationality; 3) derogatory information,[14] if applicable, including but not limited to wants and warrants, KSTs, sexual offender registration, and immigration violations; 4) IDENT watchlist status information; 5) miscellaneous officer comment information; 6) document information and identifiers (e.g., passport and visa data, document type, document number, and country of issuance); and 7) current and historic whereabouts.

Encounter data: transaction identifier data (sending organization; timestamp; workstation; reason fingerprinted, such as entry, visa application, credentialing application, or apprehension; and any available encounter information, including an IDENT-generated encounter identification number).

Test and training data: biometric data that may be real or simulated and biographic and encounter-related data for use only by US-VISIT personnel for testing and training purposes.

2.2 What are the sources of the information and how is the information collected for the project?

Information is collected by DHS components, DoS (information for visas and background investigations), DOJ, DOD, other federal, state, local, tribal, and foreign governments, foreign law enforcement agencies, and noncriminal justice origins.[15]

IDENT data providers collect the information differently depending on their authorities and mission. These collection methods include:

- Directly from the individual via an application for an immigration benefit, background investigation, at a Port of Entry, or a credential;

- Via direct encounters or forensic data gathering from military operations and intelligence operations;

---

[14] A set of data related to negative or criminal information associated with an encounter.

[15] Non-criminal justice data providers are defined as those who use criminal history records for purposes authorized by Federal or State law other than purposes relating to criminal justice activities, including employment suitability, licensing determinations, immigration and naturalization matters, and national security clearances. 42 U.S.C. § 14616.

- Indirectly, such as in the case of information through records shared by foreign governments according to written agreement or cooperative arrangement; or

- Directly or indirectly from the individual during a law enforcement action.

The data may be collected by IDENT data providers through an online application, a paper-based application, a mobile biometric device, a fixed platform, or in-person interviews. Latent prints may be manually collected at a crime scene and/or another site relevant to the work of an IDENT user such as the site of a terrorist incident. The data is then securely transmitted to IDENT where it is used to support the DHS mission.

All DHS sources and major external sources of IDENT data are explained below. A more detailed accounting of external sources is provided in the appendices of this document.

DHS Sources

CBP: CBP officers are responsible for screening all international travelers[16] to the United States. As part of the screening process, CBP officers collect digital fingerprints and a digital photograph from non-U.S. citizen travelers as required:

- At primary inspection points entering the U.S. at air and sea POEs with limited exceptions;
- Upon referral to secondary inspection[17] crossing U.S. land borders; and/or
- In advance of border crossing through an application and approved enrollment in a trusted traveler program.

CBP's trusted traveler programs provide expedited transit for pre-approved, low-risk international travelers through dedicated U.S. border POEs. CBP is therefore able to expedite the inspection and security process for these lower risk travelers and allow more scrutiny for those travelers who present a higher risk. U.S. or certain non-U.S. citizen travelers can apply for membership in a trusted traveler program, including NEXUS, Secure Electronic Network for Travelers Rapid Inspection (SENTRI), Free and Secure Trade (FAST), and Global Entry (GE) through CBP's Global Online Enrollment System (GOES).[18] The data is stored in the Global Enrollment System (GES) and transmitted to IDENT. IDENT maintains the fingerprints—prints from each of the traveler's border crossings as well as 10 prints from the initial vetting process—and limited identity (such as name and date of birth) and border-crossing information. When a traveler crosses the U.S. border at a POE, he or she provides four prints, typically using an unstaffed, automated kiosk. The four prints are sent to IDENT to verify that they belong to the same individual who was initially approved as a trusted traveler and enrolled in the GES program, and to determine that the individual continues to have no derogatory information that would make them ineligible to continue participating in the trusted traveler program.

---

[16] A full list of exceptions is listed on the DHS website at http://www.dhs.gov/files/programs/editorial_0527.shtm.
[17] Secondary inspection is the interview area at a Port of Entry where CBP inspectors conduct additional research on an individual traveler in order to verify information without causing delays for other arriving passengers.
[18] See Global Online Enrollment System PIA at
http://www.dhs.gov/xlibrary/assets/privacy/privacy_pia_cbp_goes.pdf.

Finally, US-VISIT and CBP have conducted three limited Biometric Exit pilots using self-service kiosks and mobile capture solutions to obtain fingerprints from individuals immediately prior to their departure from the United States. While the pilots have been completed the data collected are retained in IDENT. In addition, in July 2012, CBP began a six-week pilot program to collect iris scans of individuals apprehended by CBP Border Patrol at the McAllen, Texas, Border Patrol Station. [19]

ICE: ICE collects information from individuals encountered/arrested for criminal and/or immigration violations and provides this information to IDENT through the course of an investigation, arrest, booking, detention, and/or removal from the United States. ICE also collects information from foreign countries on individuals of interest. As part of its overstay process, US-VISIT incorporates the FIN in IDENT with information in the Arrival and Departure Information System (ADIS)[20] to identify individuals who may have overstayed the authorized terms of their admission. US-VISIT provides this information to ICE for appropriate enforcement action.

USCG: The USCG interdicts and refers for prosecution illegal immigrants and migrant smugglers off the coast of the U.S. The USCG cutter personnel use mobile biometric collection devices to fingerprint individuals. The information is sent via email over a satellite link to IDENT. The USCG Central Command Center submits queries directly to the IDENT database and receives the responses. Following successful receipt of each biometric record, US-VISIT compares the biometric information against IDENT and DHS accessed databases and communicates a "Hit" or "No Match" response to the Coast Guard. Relevant criminal history information is available to Coast Guard and DHS decision makers to consider with respect to disposition of interdicted persons (e.g., repatriation, referral for prosecution, etc.).

In addition, USCG conducts boarding operations to confirm identities of crew aboard High Interest Vessels.

USCIS: USCIS uses IDENT to establish and verify the identities of individuals applying, and being adjudicated for immigration benefits, including asylum or refugee status. USCIS collects information from individuals applying for immigration benefits and petitions, including asylum, refugee, and naturalization, and inter-country adoption.

External U.S. Government Sources (Non-DHS U.S. Government Sources)

Federal, State, Local, Tribal and International agencies: Latent fingerprints are collected by federal, state, local, tribal and international agencies for investigative and national security purposes. The use of latent prints whether submitted by DOJ, DOD, or state, tribal or local law enforcement helps US-VISIT and its general border security mission by improving IDENT's ability to identify individuals. These agencies collect latent prints and send them to US-VISIT for a search of IDENT. Latent fingerprints are stored in IDENT's Unsolved Latent File (ULF). A latent print can be searched against and enrolled in IDENT's ULF. Once enrolled in the IDENT ULF, a latent print is available for subsequent searches with known prints as new biometric encounters are enrolled in IDENT. Latent print collection is useful for supporting the DHS mission of keeping our nation secure.

---

[19] See CBP Portal (E3) to Enforce/IDENT at http://www.dhs.gov/xlibrary/assets/privacy/privacy-pia-cbp-e3.pdf.
[20] See ADIS PIA at: http://www.dhs.gov/xlibrary/assets/privacy/privacy_pia_usvisit_adis_2007.pdf.

For example, a state law enforcement officer is investigating a crime scene involving a deceased victim and collects a latent print from the scene. The latent print is believed to belong to the perpetrator of the crime, but the identity of the perpetrator is unknown. The latent print is checked against IDENT without results; the print is then enrolled in IDENT. The owner of the prints fled the country after committing the crime. The perpetrator, after a period of time, attempts to re-enter the United States and is apprehended by the Border Patrol. The Border Patrol Agent submits the subject's prints to IDENT and receives the latent match. The Border Patrol Agent processes the subject for removal proceedings, thus supporting the DHS mission, and contacts the state law enforcement agency submitting the latent print and turns the subject over to face the appropriate charges.

DoS: DoS uses IDENT to establish and verify the identities of visa applicants at embassies and consulates around the world through its BioVisa program. Consular officers use this information in determining visa eligibility. DoS also collects information from in-scope visa applicants and information on behalf of USCIS for expatriate U.S. citizens adopting foreign-born children abroad. Finally, DoS collects information from individuals seeking access to DoS facilities (i.e., for employment).

DOD and the Intelligence Community: US-VISIT is working across the federal government to promote intelligence efforts in identifying high-risk individuals. DOD collects information to support its military mission, detainee affairs, and force protection efforts as well as its antiterrorism, special operations, stability operations, homeland defense, counterintelligence, and intelligence efforts around the world. Additionally, DOD enrolls information collected from non-U.S. citizens denied access to military posts. This information may be shared with US-VISIT biometric services to facilitate identification of terrorists. Finally, DOD uses IDENT to help identify KSTs by matching against known and latent fingerprints collected from terrorist safe houses and ongoing criminal investigations.

DOJ and Local Law Enforcement: Criminal justice agencies use IDENT to ensure that they have accurate identity information about individuals they arrest or have under investigation for a crime. DHS and the FBI have established interoperability between IDENT and the FBI's IAFIS fingerprint database. DHS has published a separate DHS-DOJ Interoperability PIA detailing IDENT-IAFIS Interoperability.[21] Information is collected through DHS-DOJ interoperability users for national security, law enforcement, immigration and border management, and intelligence purposes, and to conduct background investigations for national security positions and certain positions of public trust.

<u>**External Foreign Sources:**</u>

Information collected by foreign partners that is shared with the U.S. government is collected by law enforcement and immigration officials and protected by international agreements, U.S. laws, and additional implementation agreements and established protocols. The details of sharing with each external foreign source are outlined in the appendices to this PIA.

---

[21] For a full discussion of DHS-DOJ interoperability, see DHS/NPPD/USVISIT/PIA-007 Biometric Interoperability Between the U.S. Department of Homeland Security and the U.S. Department of Justice PIA at www.dhs.gov/privacy.

INTERPOL: Information from INTERPOL in IDENT includes INTERPOL fingerprint files for valid INTERPOL notices issued since January 2002. These include fingerprints for wanted, missing, and deceased persons, persons with criminal histories, and persons of interest to law enforcement authorities. The INTERPOL – U.S. National Central Bureau (USNCB) provides this data to US-VISIT to assist in identifying fugitives and wanted persons attempting to enter the United States, and to otherwise assist U.S. law enforcement officials in performing their official duties. The details of sharing with INTERPOL are outlined in the DHS-DOJ Interoperability PIA.

Five Country Conference: The Five Country Conference (FCC) is a forum for cooperation on migration and border security between the countries of Australia, Canada, New Zealand, the United Kingdom, and the United States (collectively called the FCC partners). FCC partners, including the United States, exchange biometric information in specific immigration cases where:

- the identity of the individual is unknown or uncertain;
- the individual's whereabouts are unknown; or
- there is reason to suspect that the person has been encountered by a FCC partner country.

The biometrics are exchanged to search against the existing biometric holdings of each FCC partner for determining the existence of information that may be pertinent to immigration and border management decision makers.

Preventing and Combating Serious Crime: In 2008, the U.S. began signing Preventing and Combating Serious Crime (PCSC) agreements primarily with countries that participate or seek to participate in the Visa Waiver Program (VWP). The agreements formalize the sharing of biometric and biographic data for the purposes of preventing and combating serious crime. The details of sharing are outlined in PCSC related appendices attached to this PIA.

2.3 Does the project use information from commercial sources or publicly available data? If so, explain why and how this information is used.

IDENT does not use information from commercial sources or publicly available data.

2.4 Discuss how accuracy of the data is ensured.

Information is collected directly from an individual during an immigration and border management, credentialing, law enforcement, or military operations encounter to ensure accuracy at collection. In some instances, an additional check for accuracy is part of the collection process (such as in the immigration benefits biometric collection process.)

A 10-fingerprint collection standard, which superseded a 2-fingerprint standard for user applications and for storage within IDENT, was initially developed to improve the accuracy of biometric identification and fingerprint-matching capabilities. This standard includes capturing all 10 fingerprints from travelers at the earliest possible interaction for identification purposes, and fewer than all 10 fingerprints for subsequent verifications. Collecting more fingerprints increases the system's fingerprint-matching accuracy, reducing the possibility that the system will misidentify an individual.

Identification with all 10 fingerprints enables more accurate and comprehensive searches against IDENT. This also improves the quality of data associated with an individual, and it decreases the chance of false negative and false positive matches. The identification capability facilitates rapid searching across the complete fingerprint repository to determine whether the subject was previously enrolled in the IDENT system.

The verification capability allows IDENT to perform a 1:1 verification of biometric data to establish whether the subject is the same individual whose fingerprints were formerly submitted and are stored in IDENT. Identifications and verifications are fingerprint-based and do not use biographic information, such as name and date of birth, which may be fraudulent.

Additional accuracy processes are built in to the process for matching IDENT records against latent fingerprints, which are prints collected at serious crime scenes and/or terrorist incidents, for example, and run against IDENT to identify individuals of law enforcement or national security interest. Because these prints may be partial, incomplete, or oriented differently than in controlled collection (in addition to many other possibly anomalies), accurate identification is more difficult. To ensure accurate matches for latent prints, IDENT returns a number of possible matches to trained and experienced fingerprint examiners in its Biometrics Support Center (BSC). BSC latent-print examiners make a final determination on whether the submitted print matches any of the fingerprints currently retained in IDENT. If BSC examiners confirm that there is a match in IDENT, the submitting agency can request additional information on the individual.

Individuals who believe that the data held on them in IDENT is inaccurate can submit a redress request for a review and correction of that inaccurate data. For more information refer to section 7.0 on redress.

2.5   **Privacy Impact Analysis: Related to Characterization of the Information**

Privacy Risk: There is a risk that the quality and integrity of information that will be collected and maintained in IDENT may not meet the standards required to serve its purpose of biometric and biographic verification and matching, thus potentially causing misidentification. Because US-VISIT does not collect the information provided, the processing and storage of data in IDENT is dependent on the appropriate and accurate data fields of incoming records, which have been identified to correspond with IDENT data fields as described.

Mitigation: IDENT performs certain quality checks (e.g., determining the quality of a captured fingerprint and its suitability for matching in the future) and seeks to ensure that the data meets a minimum level of quality and completeness. However, it is ultimately the responsibility of the original data owner, whether an organization external or internal to DHS, to ensure the accuracy, completeness, and quality of the data.

Privacy Risk: Data collected by mobile devices is susceptible to unauthorized monitoring, interception, and tampering during the transmittal process.

Mitigation: To minimize these risks, data is encrypted on the mobile devices used and in the transmittal process, using standards, policies, and procedures established by NIST and DHS.

Privacy Risk: There is a risk of collecting more information than is required for the purposes of the system, because IDENT collects biographic data that details the subject's encounters, which is not strictly necessary for identification.

Mitigation: Depending upon the data user, IDENT shares different levels of responses. For certain data providers, the full encounter history of an individual's biometric interactions with the Department is required to meet the mission of the agency. For example, as a data provider, CBP requires the retention of travel data to identify and record international travelers' entry into the U.S. at ports of entry as part of its inspection process. As owner of this data, CBP determines whether its non-derogatory information should be shared with IDENT users. When CBP determines that the user does not need and/or is not authorized to receive this travel data, it is withheld from the response IDENT provides to the IDENT user. The IDENT response is appropriately scoped to the purpose of each authorized user.

Privacy Risk: In a limited number of instances, the automated biometric match process will result in biometric information that does not correctly map to one individual. This can occur, for example, when an individual has low quality fingerprints, which increases the likelihood of a matching error and causes the system to establish two identities for one person.

Mitigation: This risk is mitigated in two ways. Internally, a process called "merge on the fly" can automatically merge records where the same person has two different identities in IDENT, usually because of poor fingerprint quality. The process works when a new encounter matches to two identities in the system, indicating that the two identities are in fact one person. When the new encounter is tied to two separate identities, the system automatically merges them into one identity as part of the matching process. In other instances, the individual knows that the wrong biographic information has been assigned to them, either because of an error in automation or because of a human error such as an inspector transposing the traveler's biometrics with their travel companion's biographics. When the traveler is able to identify the problem and request a redress of the error, he or she can apply to the US-VISIT Privacy Office to have that information corrected once the error is verified. Alternatively, to correct inaccurate or erroneous information believed to reside in IDENT, individuals, regardless of citizenship, should submit redress requests online through the DHS Traveler Redress Inquiry Program (TRIP). DHS TRIP is a single point of contact for individuals who have inquiries or seek resolution regarding difficulties they experienced during their travel screening at transportation hubs—like airports and train stations—or crossing U.S. borders.

Privacy Risk: There is a risk that latent fingerprints collected at crime scenes from individuals who are not perpetrators may be retained inappropriately and indefinitely in IDENT.

Mitigation: Latent prints from individuals who were deemed victims, bystanders, witnesses, and/or those handling the evidence at criminal or terrorist incidents are not to be retained in IDENT once they are identified to US-VISIT by the providing agency. Also, any latent prints that are identified are removed from the ULF.

Section 3.0 Uses of the Information

The following questions require a clear description of the project's use of information.

3.1 Describe how and why the project uses the information.

IDENT is the central DHS-wide system for the storage and processing of biometric and associated biographic information for the purposes of national security, law enforcement, immigration and border management, intelligence, and credentialing (e.g., background investigations for national security positions and certain positions of public trust), as well as for providing associated testing, training, management reporting, planning and analysis, or other administrative uses. IDENT receives biometric and biographic data from DHS and external users to conduct biometric searches against IDENT. Most IDENT users opt to have IDENT search for biometric matches of their data and also enroll that data as new encounters into IDENT. Alternatively, they may choose to search only but not enroll or search and enroll only if the identity already exists in IDENT. DHS only enrolls data in IDENT that may be used to support the DHS mission. IDENT serves as a biographic and biometric repository for the Department. As a data steward, US-VISIT provides a service to its data providers and data users. US-VISIT identifies each collection by data provider and its authority to use, retain, and share it. IDENT enables sharing with authorized users after the data provider has approved the sharing.

US-VISIT

IDENT Biometric Watchlist Adjudication

US-VISIT's Identity Services Branch (ISB) uses IDENT, in conjunction with other government systems, to determine whether an individual should be promoted to, or demoted from the IDENT watchlist. The IDENT watchlist provides a repository of persons of interest, including but not limited to: wants and warrants from federal, state, and international law enforcement agencies through the FBI; foreign-born criminal fugitives; KSTs; deported felons, sexual offender registrants, gang-related records, subjects who have violated U.S. immigration laws, or who have been denied a BioVisa by DoS; and other persons of interest to DHS. IDENT data providers, as well as selected US-VISIT staff (such as those assigned to the visa overstay program) provide the data and indicate whether the particular individual should be included in the IDENT watchlist in accordance with standard operating procedures that include reviews of data provided and confirmation that it meets established watchlist criteria. IDENT users do not use the IDENT watchlist to make a final determination; the watchlist is only used to flag individuals who may be of interest to individual US-VISIT users. Further analysis is conducted by those users upon a match in IDENT pursuant to their specific programmatic authorities.

ISB analysts search a number of DHS systems, including ADIS,[22] and external systems, to determine whether a subject is eligible to be removed from the watchlist. IDENT is used as a source by analysts; it provides them with the necessary information regarding why an individual is on the IDENT watchlist. If the analyst determines that the individual should no longer be on the IDENT watchlist, the

---

[22] For a full discussion of ADIS, see the ADIS PIA located at:
http://www.dhs.gov/files/publications/gc_1281125467696.shtm#44.

analyst will demote the individual to reflect that the individual was removed from the IDENT watchlist.

Overstays

A primary function of US-VISIT is to identify lawfully-admitted non-immigrants who remain in the United States beyond their authorized periods of stay. If individuals remain in the United States for longer than their allotted time, this can have a bearing on their right to remain in the country or receive benefits. ISB analysts use IDENT, in conjunction with various government systems, to help determine if an individual is either an in-country overstay (an individual who remained in the United States and has exceeded his or her period of admission) or an out-of-country overstay (an individual who has left the country, but who exceeded his or her period of admission while in the United States.) ISB analysts use IDENT to gather information on the individual. ISB analysts use the information in IDENT against other systems to gather all the necessary information about the individual to determine whether the subject is an overstay. IDENT, through the interface Secondary Inspection Tool, (SIT), specifically provides the analyst with the FIN, IDENT watchlist information, complete name, DOB, citizenship, gender, and travel document information. IDENT can also provide details about benefits for which the individual has applied. This assists the analyst in determining the status of the individual and what additional systems should be reviewed for more information on the individual.

Latent Identification

The US-VISIT BSC receives requests from federal, state, local, tribal, and international law enforcement agencies for the identification of latent fingerprints. Agencies can submit latent fingerprints extracted from serious crime scenes and/or terrorist events and ask the BSC to search against the fingerprints retained in IDENT.[23] All incoming new 10 prints are run against the ULF. This coordination directly supports the DHS mission, as it enables DHS to identify individuals who may pose a threat to the United States and should be inadmissible or denied a benefit. BSC latent print examiners make a final determination on whether the submitted print matches any of the fingerprints currently retained in IDENT. If BSC examiners confirm that there is a match in IDENT, the submitting agency can request additional information on the individual. The majority of latent prints in the ULF come from DoD and FBI, while the remaining come from DHS, state, and local law enforcement. US-VISIT requires that state and local law enforcement submit latents only for serious crimes, preferably after running them through IAFIS. US-VISIT retains latent prints that are not initially identified for future searches against known prints to support the DHS mission, unless the latent print contributor requests that the prints not be retained. Depending on the requesting user's needs and written agreements, the latent prints may be enrolled or used as search-only data. Latent prints from individuals who were deemed victims, bystanders and/or those handling the evidence at criminal or terrorist incidents are not to be retained in IDENT once they are identified to US-VISIT by the providing agency. State and Local Law enforcement agencies inform DHS once they identify individuals, or determine that they are bystanders/witnesses.

---

[23] Through latent-print interoperability, agencies submitting fingerprints will be able to simultaneously search IDENT and the FBI's IAFIS for the identification and verification of latent fingerprints. DHS-DOJ interoperability PIA is currently being updated to include a discussion on latent print interoperability.

Redress

In coordination with ISB, the US-VISIT Privacy Office uses IDENT to respond to redress requests. The US-VISIT Privacy Office and ISB use IDENT, concurrently with ADIS, to research US-VISIT records on individuals who have submitted redress requests and to correct any information that may be inaccurate. For example, if an individual has a fingerprint record or FIN incorrectly linked to another person's record, the next time he or she enters the United States the individual may be sent to secondary inspection, which can cause inconvenience and hardships. If the individual submits a redress request, the US-VISIT Privacy Office and ISB can work together to correct the issue. This will help ease the travel process for the individual the next time he or she enters the country and ensures that US-VISIT records are as accurate, complete, and up-to-date as possible.

CBP

US-VISIT helps establish and verify the identities of international visitors arriving at air, sea, and land border POEs. The CBP Office of Field Operations (OFO) uses IDENT at primary and secondary inspection points within air, sea, and land POEs. At primary inspection, CBP OFO reads a travel document number electronically and IDENT conducts a "look-up" to determine how many prints should be collected. Based on the travel document scanned, if a person has already submitted prints in the past and the identity is known to IDENT, then only four prints are collected. This saves CBP processing time. Ten prints are collected for identities that are new to IDENT or for those who have not submitted prints in the past. IDENT verifies an individual's identity and returns a response indicating whether or not derogatory information exists for that individual. If an individual is referred to secondary inspection, the agent will review the full IDENT response through SIT, or through a system to system interface, along with responses from other database searches, and make an admissibility determination. This allows the officer to gather pertinent IDENT watchlist and previous-encounter information for the purposes of determining admissibility.

Through CBP's Global Enrollment System (GES), an applicant can apply for one of the trusted-traveler programs, such as NEXUS, SENTRI, FAST, and GE. These programs assess an individual's risk level as a traveler and provide benefits if that risk is deemed to be low. Individuals can submit an online application or can apply by mail. The data is stored in GES and transmitted to IDENT. IDENT maintains the fingerprints— prints from each border crossing as well as 10 prints from the initial vetting process——and limited identity (name and date of birth) and border-crossing information. When a traveler crosses a border, at the Port of Entry he or she provides four prints, typically using an unstaffed, automated kiosk. The four prints are sent to IDENT to verify that they belong to the same individual who was initially approved as a trusted traveler and enrolled in the program.

CBP's Office of Border Patrol (OBP) uses IDENT to identify individuals attempting to enter the United States between land ports of entry. Individuals are stopped by CBP OBP and taken to Border Patrol stations or other processing areas where 10 prints are taken. IDENT returns an identification response that includes the full IDENT response.

CBP and other DHS entities may use IDENT for the purpose of preventing and combating serious crime where they may send a request to US-VISIT to extract biometrics from IDENT on a subject of interest to send forward to the foreign partner (who has signed a PCSC agreement) to query that country's systems.

In an effort to develop the technology and processes necessary to support additional biometric modalities, CBP and US-VISIT are currently developing the Multimodal Limited Production Pilot (LPP) for which CBP will collect biometrics (iris scans) and biographics via mobile devices at the border patrol station in McAllen, TX. The results of the LPP will set the stage to define the multimodal Initial Operating Capability and the Full Operating Capability.

USCG

USCG interdicts and refers for prosecutions illegal immigrants and migrant smugglers off the coast of the United States and uses IDENT data to identify individuals and confirm immigration status if the individual has documentation. USCG cutter personnel use mobile biometric collection devices to fingerprint individuals. They also place a numbered wrist strap on the individual to identify them. The information is sent via e-mail over a satellite link. The USCG Central Command Center submits queries directly to the IDENT database and receives responses.

In addition, USCG conducts boarding operations to confirm the identities of crew members aboard high-interest vessels.

USCIS

USCIS collects information from immigrant benefit applicants. When an applicant reports to an Application Support Center (ASC), which is a USCIS facility where applicants apply for benefit applications, he or she is fingerprinted and biographics are collected through the benefit application process. The fingerprints are sent to IDENT and searches are returned. At follow-up visits, the USCIS adjudicator performs a 1:1 verification using SIT, which allows for the capture and submission of fingerprints for verification.

For refugee applicants, the information may be collected at refugee camps and transmitted to an ASC for processing and submission to IDENT.

ICE

ICE has the authority to enforce a variety of customs and immigration laws, and makes arrests for criminal and administrative violations of those laws. ICE uses a system known as the Enforcement Integrated Database (EID) to create a booking record for those arrested by ICE.[24] ICE enrolls the arrestee's biometric and biographic information in IDENT via an interface between EID and IDENT. At the same time, ICE also searches IDENT and the FBI's IAFIS via DHS-DOJ interoperability, to identify or verify the identity of the arrestee and to determine if additional derogatory information exists or if there are outstanding wants or warrants. IDENT uses the information to create a new encounter, which is identified under an ICE organizational code in IDENT.

---

[24] See the DHS/ICE/PIA -015(d) Enforcement Integrated Database (EID) ENFORCE Alien Removal Module Update, April 6, 2012.

In agreements with foreign partners, ICE also enrolls in IDENT the biometric and biographic information of persons of interest obtained by foreign immigration and law enforcement agencies during immigration and law enforcement encounters and operations. The information pertains to aliens who are criminals or known or suspected gang members, and aliens from countries known to support terrorism or violent extremism. ICE and other agencies also use the information during screening to identify persons who may require further review during a visa application or border inspection process. ICE uses the information to run queries against IDENT to find relevant matches to initiate investigations into international fugitives and Extra-Territorial Criminal Travel (ECT) networks. Additionally, US-VISIT forwards overstay analysis to ICE for further review. ICE's Counterterrorism and Criminal Exploitation Unit is also capable of initiating its own overstay analysis and enforcement.

ICE may send a request to US-VISIT to extract biometrics from IDENT on a subject of interest to send to a foreign partner who has signed the PCSC agreement to query their systems. For instance, if ICE has an open investigation on a subject that has a nexus to a country that has signed the PCSC agreement, ICE can use IDENT to send the biometrics of the subject of the open investigation.

During casework investigations, ICE may also use IDENT to search latent prints.

3.2 Does the project use technology to conduct electronic searches, queries, or analyses in an electronic database to discover or locate a predictive pattern or an anomaly? If so, state how DHS plans to use such results.

IDENT does not conduct searching, querying, or analysis to discover or locate a predictive pattern or anomaly in the data.

3.3 Are there other components with assigned roles and responsibilities within the system?

As described in the IDENT data users section within DHS, CBP, USCG, ICE, USCIS, and US-VISIT have access to IDENT. Data from IDENT may be disclosed to IDENT users through the following means:

1. Data from IDENT may be transmitted between IDENT and other DHS systems through direct system-to-system interfaces.

2. Internal DHS IDENT users may use an IDENT interface known as SIT. SIT shows biographic encounter data in a matched IDENT record, based on retrieval with an identifying number. Certain IDENT users with permission may also see the biometrics. SIT also provides the capability to capture biographic and biometric data and provide it to IDENT for a comparison to the biometrics associated with previous encounter data enrolled in IDENT. This process is called 1:1 verification. The search parameters of SIT only allow for one record at a time to be searched and displayed for any particular user.

3. US-VISIT also receives *ad hoc* identification requests from domestic and international law enforcement agencies and foreign governments to assist in immigration processes, active law enforcement investigations, national security incidents, and intelligence activities, or for preventing or combating serious crime. The requests may be received via e-mail, fax, telephone, mail, or some other means in a secure manner. For *ad hoc* requests, the user receives results via encrypted e-mail or by other secure means. Other types of transmission or disclosure may be required in some circumstances to meet the mission needs of the stakeholder.

3.4 <u>Privacy Impact Analysis</u>: Related to the Uses of Information

<u>Privacy Risk</u>: There is a risk that DHS IDENT users may use information for purposes inconsistent with the purpose of the original collection.

<u>Mitigation</u>: US-VISIT established the Identity Capabilities Working Group (ICWG), which is chaired by US-VISIT and includes representatives from each data-sharing partner. Change requests to IDENT must be reviewed and approved by the ICWG. This allows the ICWG members to identify risks to their subsequent programs and processes and to provide input for mitigation before the deployment of new capabilities and uses.

Section 4.0 Notice

The following questions seek information about the project's notice to the individual about the information collected, the right to consent to uses of said information, and the right to decline to provide information.

4.1 How does the project provide individuals notice prior to the collection of information? If notice is not provided, explain why not.

Federal, foreign, state and local government entities that contribute data to IDENT are referred to as IDENT data providers.

IDENT providers may contribute data to IDENT in one of two ways:

- *Search and Enroll:* The data provider provides data it collects to conduct an IDENT search and enrolls that data as a new IDENT encounter.

- *Search and Assign:* The data provider provides data it collects to conduct an IDENT search, and enrolls as a new IDENT encounter only if another encounter already exists. These data providers cannot create a new identity in IDENT; they can only add encounters to an already existing identity.

IDENT data providers provide direct notice to individuals prior to collection, when possible. All DHS components provide general notice through the publication of PIAs and SORNs. CBP provides notice via forms collected at primary inspection and through trusted-traveler applications. USCG personnel distribute to all persons interdicted at sea copies of a standard notification of biometrics collection, including a description of the uses of biometric information and contact information for redress. USCIS provides notice in the application instructions for immigration benefits. Notice prior to the collection of information by ICE or CBP may be limited or nonexistent because of the law enforcement and customs and immigration purposes for which the information is collected. Individuals may be notified by other law enforcement agencies at the point of collection of the original data that their information may be shared for law enforcement purposes. In the case of latent fingerprints, individuals will not be notified of the collection.

Background check applications and applications for credentials contain notices that discuss the purpose and use of a particular collection. In addition, notice is provided to individuals through the publication of this IDENT PIA and SORN in the Federal Register. Notice is also provided through the publication of PIAs and SORNs of the underlying systems of original collection. Certain national security and law enforcement collections may not provide notice because to do so would jeopardize the ability to conduct an investigation.

4.2 What opportunities are available for individuals to consent to uses, decline to provide information, or opt out of the project?

Individuals have the right to decline to provide data to DHS components, DoS, DOJ, and DOD, unless they are part of a law enforcement action. However, in doing so, they may become ineligible for any benefits for which they are applying. Once they have provided the information, individuals have no opportunity to consent to or refuse the use of this data for national security, law enforcement, immigration, intelligence, and other homeland security mission-related purposes.

Additionally, once the collected data, regardless of source, are stored in IDENT it will be used for national security, law enforcement, immigration, intelligence, and other homeland security mission-related purposes, as defined by DHS, and as described in the IDENT SORN. The data maintained in IDENT and shared with authorized IDENT users has previously been collected from DHS components, DoS, DOJ, DOD, state, local, and foreign government agencies. Individuals seeking federal or other employment requiring a background security investigation provide specific consent for the search of all necessary records at the time of application.

4.3 Privacy Impact Analysis: Related to Notice

Privacy Risk: There is a risk that an individual may not be aware that information collected directly from them (e.g., provided during an application for a benefit or credential) is shared with and stored in the IDENT data providers' databases.

Mitigation: By publishing this PIA, the DHS-DOJ Interoperability PIA, and the corresponding appendices, US-VISIT provides notice of the uses of information. This risk is additionally mitigated by the fact that in many cases, the person submitting information is providing it directly to DHS. The collecting agency provides notice at the point of collection that the information may be shared with other federal, state, local, and foreign government agencies and authorized organizations following approved routine uses described in the associated published SORNs. Additionally, DHS components provide notice that information will be shared with IDENT in their PIAs. External agencies may also provide notice through PIAs. For information collected by foreign government agencies and shared by IDENT data providers with IDENT, this risk is mitigated to differing degrees depending on what notification mechanisms may be used by those original collectors.

Privacy Risk: There is a risk that individuals are not aware that their information is indirectly collected (e.g., latent fingerprints). Due to the nature of latent fingerprints, individuals whose fingerprints are collected at crime scenes and/or terrorist incidents will not be given notice.

Mitigation: This PIA, the corresponding appendices, and related PIAs provide notice of the uses of information. As addressed in Section 5.2, although individuals may not be aware that their fingerprints were extracted from crime scenes and/or terrorist incidents, latent prints from individuals who were deemed victims, bystanders, and/or those handling the evidence at crime or terrorist incidents are not to be retained in IDENT once they are identified. Moreover, state and local law enforcement agencies inform DHS once they determine that certain prints belong to victims or bystanders. DHS then removes those prints from IDENT.

Section 5.0 Data Retention by the project

The following questions are intended to outline how long the project retains the information after the initial collection.

5.1   Explain how long and for what reason the information is retained.

IDENT records are retained for 75 years. The 75-year retention period is necessary to support the holding of biometrics of subjects of interest in immigration and border management or law enforcement activities. Records shared with foreign governments may be kept by those countries for longer or shorter periods, according to the laws of those countries. DHS is re-evaluating the current retention policy to determine whether a new retention period or combination of retention periods is appropriate. DHS will publish a PIA update for any change in the retention period.

5.2   <u>Privacy Impact Analysis</u>: Related to Retention

Privacy Risk: As an INS legacy system, the retention period for IDENT was established when the system was used primarily for holding the biometrics of subjects of interest in immigration and border management or law enforcement activities. However, as a DHS-wide repository of biometrics for any of its missions, IDENT now holds data that may not need to be held for 75 years.

Mitigation: DHS is currently undertaking a re-evaluation of the retention policy and may determine a new retention period or a combination of retention periods depending on the data collected. A PIA update will be published to cover any change in the retention period.

Privacy Risk: There is a risk that latent fingerprints collected at crime scenes from individuals who are not perpetrators may be retained inappropriately in IDENT.

Mitigation: Latent prints from individuals who were deemed victims, bystanders, and/or those handling the evidence at criminal or terrorist incidents are not to be retained in IDENT once they are identified to US-VISIT by the providing agency.

Section 6.0 Information Sharing

The following questions are intended to describe the scope of the project information sharing external to the Department. External sharing encompasses sharing with other federal, state and local government, and private sector entities.

6.1 Is information shared outside of DHS as part of the normal agency operations? If so, identify the organization(s) and how the information is accessed and how it is to be used.

US-VISIT shares information with federal, state, local, tribal, foreign, and international agencies for national security, law enforcement, criminal justice, immigration and border management, and intelligence purposes, as well as to conduct background investigations for national security positions and certain positions of public trust. System-to-system external IDENT users are discussed in full in the attached appendices. IDENT connectivity through interoperability is discussed in the DHS-DOJ Interoperability and the forthcoming DHS-DOD Interoperability PIAs.

Depending on the agreements in place, IDENT users may receive a full IDENT response in answer to a biometric search request or a limited response. DHS and the data owners make the final determination on the type of response and the amount of data an IDENT user should receive. The content of IDENT response messages is derived from individual encounters submitted by a variety of IDENT data owners, based on agreements to share by those IDENT data owners and the interest of the data recipient.

6.2 Describe how the external sharing noted in 6.1 is compatible with the SORN noted in 1.2.

The IDENT SORN Routine Use "H" covers the sharing of information with federal, state, local, tribal, foreign, and international agencies for national security, law enforcement, immigration and border management, and intelligence purposes. This is compatible with the original collection as determined by the data owner. The data owner dictates how NPPD/US-VISIT shares the information externally to ensure that the external sharing is compatible with the purpose of the original collection

The IDENT SORN Routine Use "I" covers the sharing of information with federal, state, local, tribal, foreign, and international agencies to conduct background investigations for national security positions and certain positions of public trust. The data owner collects the information and dictates how the information is shared externally. The data owner ensures compatibility between the collection and external sharing.

Please see appendices for details on how each instance of external sharing is compatible with the IDENT SORN. US-VISIT is currently reviewing and updating the IDENT SORN.

6.3   Does the project place limitations on re-dissemination?

All MOUs and information-sharing access agreements that govern the sharing of IDENT information include limitations on re-dissemination. These limitations will be discussed in full in the attached external IDENT users' appendices.

6.4   Describe how the project maintains a record of any disclosures outside of the Department.

US-VISIT retains an accounting of records disclosed outside of the Department. The disclosures include records that are paper-based or electronic and record the date, nature, and purpose of each dissemination and disclosure, along with the name and address of the individual or agency to which the disclosure is made. This list of disclosures is retained as part of the accounting requirements for the IDENT system in order to be able to recreate the information to demonstrate compliance.

IDENT maintains an audit record in the database for each system message sent to an external agency. Audit logs are maintained by the IDENT Operations and Maintenance (O&M) Team and the Information Technology Management Branch. Access to audit logs is limited strictly to core O&M personnel. The audit log data is backed up regularly as part of the overall IDENT database backup and archiving process.

6.5   Privacy Impact Analysis: Related to Information Sharing

Privacy Risk: Because of the sensitivity of certain classes of individuals' data collected by DHS components, there is a potential risk that sensitive data may be shared with groups not authorized to receive the data.

Mitigation: The IDENT system incorporates a robust filtering process based off the data owners' requirements for all information sharing. An IDENT data provider may inform US-VISIT of limitations on dissemination in the data sharing agreement or though the ICWG. IDENT filtering capabilities ensure that data is only shared with data provider-approved agencies for approved purposes.

US-VISIT is currently working on additional filtering capabilities to ensure that information about certain special protected classes of individuals is protected.

Privacy Risk: There is a risk that IDENT users who have not yet been approved as an IDENT user will gain access to IDENT data through third party sharing.

Mitigation: The potential for unauthorized sharing is mitigated by implementing access controls to ensure that only authorized IDENT users can access the data, by placing limitations on third-party sharing, by limiting the amount of data shared based on specific circumstances described in information sharing access agreements, and by conducting periodic reviews, as appropriate, of the use of the data with end users. The applicable data-sharing agreements require proper new user and use authorization.

Privacy Risk: There is a risk that IDENT provides users more information than is minimally necessary for their authorized purpose.

Mitigation: Being an authorized user does not provide automatic access to all of an individual's IDENT records. For example, organization-level data filtering is applied to encounter data, which allows for certain data (for example, asylum data) to be protected so that only approved organizations will be able to access the data. Individual data owners provide the restrictions regarding the sharing of their data with other organizations. US-VISIT facilitates these decisions by data owners through its governance process.

Section 7.0 Redress

The following questions seek information about processes in place for individuals to seek redress which may include access to records about themselves, ensuring the accuracy of the information collected about them, and/or filing complaints.

7.1 What are the procedures that allow individuals to access their information?

In accordance with the provisions of the Privacy Act of 1974 and Freedom of Information Act (FOIA), the procedures that allow individuals to access information in a DHS system of records are posted on the DHS public-facing website: http://www.dhs.gov/xfoia/editorial_0579.shtm.

Individuals can request access to their records by contacting: US-VISIT FOIA Officer, Department of Homeland Security, 245 Murray Drive SW, Washington, DC 20598-0675. Requests for information are evaluated to ensure that any release of information is lawful; will not impede an investigation of an actual or potential criminal, civil, or regulatory violation; and will not reveal the existence of an investigation or investigative interest on the part of DHS or another agency. Access may be limited pursuant to exemptions asserted under 5 USC §§ 552a(j)(2) and (k)(2) for the IDENT system.

7.2 What procedures are in place to allow the subject individual to correct inaccurate or erroneous information?

Individuals, regardless of citizenship, should submit redress requests online through the DHS Traveler Redress Inquiry Program[25] (TRIP) website, www.dhs.gov/trip, or mail the completed form and documents to DHS TRIP, 601 South 12th Street, TSA-901, Arlington, VA 20598-6901. Completing the form online saves processing time and helps prevent data entry errors. After an individual submits a redress form, the individual will receive notification of receipt from DHS TRIP. DHS TRIP will review the redress form and will determine which component/agency will be able to respond most effectively to the submission. When a redress request is related to US-VISIT processing, DHS TRIP will coordinate with US-VISIT. US-VISIT will then review the individual's records and correct the information, if appropriate. DHS TRIP will notify the individual of the resolution of that request. Additionally, an individual may submit redress requests directly to the US-VISIT Privacy Officer (See section 7.3). If an individual is dissatisfied with the response to his or her redress inquiry, then he or she can appeal to the DHS Chief Privacy Officer, who reviews the appeal and provides final adjudication concerning the

---

[25] See the DHS Traveler Redress Inquiry Program Privacy Impact Assessment at http://www.dhs.gov/xlibrary/assets/privacy/privacy_pia_dhstrip.pdf.

matter. The DHS Chief Privacy Officer can be contacted at Chief Privacy Officer, Attn: DHS Privacy Office, Department of Homeland Security, Mailstop 0655, 245 Murray Lane, Washington, DC 20528, USA; or by fax: 1-202-343-4010. As with access amendments may be limited pursuant to exemptions asserted under 5 USC §§ 552a(j)(2) and (k)(2) for the IDENT system.

7.3 How does the project notify individuals about the procedures for correcting their information?

Individuals are advised of the procedures for correcting their information through information available on the US-VISIT website,[26] or by contacting the US-VISIT Privacy Officer, Department of Homeland Security, 245 Murray Drive SW., Washington, DC 20598-0675. Additionally, individuals are notified by publication of this DHS PIA. The redress procedures are established and operated by DHS through DHS TRIP, which can be accessed at www.dhs.gov/trip.

7.4 Privacy Impact Analysis: Related to Redress

Privacy Risk: There is a risk that individuals, particularly non-U.S. persons, may not understand how to correct incorrect information about themselves in IDENT.

Mitigation: DHS TRIP provides a redress process through a website that facilitates the submission and processing of redress requests. Any individual can request access to or correction of their PII regardless of their nationality or country of residence. This process has been described in the DHS TRIP PIA and information is available in multiple places on DHS's public website. Redress requests that come to TRIP where a traveler encountered difficulties at the POE due to information in IDENT that needs to be modified or updated, are assigned via TRIP to US-VISIT. The US-VISIT redress team along with US-VISIT's Identity Services branch, after review, then makes appropriate corrections to the IDENT record if warranted and makes that notation in TRIP.

Alternatively, an individual may submit a redress request directly to US-VISIT. The US-VISIT website displays information on the process. In addition, if an individual is dissatisfied with the response to his or her redress inquiry, then he or she can appeal to the DHS Chief Privacy Officer, who reviews the appeal and provides final adjudication concerning the matter. The DHS Chief Privacy Officer can be contacted at Chief Privacy Officer, Attn: DHS Privacy Office, Department of Homeland Security, Mailstop 0655, 245 Murray Lane, Washington, DC 20528, USA; or by fax: 1-202-343-4010

---

[26] See the US-VISIT Website at http://www.dhs.gov/files/programs/editorial_0678.shtm.

Section 8.0 Auditing and Accountability

The following questions are intended to describe technical and policy based safeguards and security measures.

8.1 How does the project ensure that the information is used in accordance with stated practices in this PIA?

IDENT secures its data by complying with the requirements of DHS information technology security policy, particularly the DHS Information Technology (IT) Security Program Handbook for Sensitive Systems (Attachment A to DHS Management Directive 4300.1). This handbook establishes a comprehensive program to provide complete information security, including directives on roles and responsibilities, management policies, operational policies, technical controls, and application rules. IDENT is periodically evaluated to ensure that it complies with these security requirements.

IDENT provides audit trail capabilities in order to monitor, log, and analyze system transactions, as well as actions and system accesses of authorized IDENT users.

As IDENT contains data from a variety of sources, collected for a variety of uses, it is necessary to institute controls so that only those individuals with a need to know are able to access that data. IDENT has a robust set of access controls, including role-based access and interfaces, which limit individual access to the appropriate discrete data collections. Misuse of the data in IDENT is mitigated by requiring that IDENT users conform to appropriate security and privacy policies, follow established rules of behavior, and be adequately trained regarding the security of their systems. Also, a periodic assessment of physical, technical, and administrative controls is performed to enhance accountability and data integrity. External connections must be documented and approved with both parties' signatures in an interconnection security agreement (ISA), which outlines controls in place to protect the confidentiality, integrity, and availability of the information being shared or processed.

8.2 Describe what privacy training is provided to users either generally or specifically relevant to the project.

DHS provides comprehensive privacy training that all DHS personnel are required to attend in person within the first 30 days of their assigned entry on duty. This follows the high-level overview privacy training provided by DHS as part of new-employee orientation. Users of DHS/US-VISIT systems, specifically the IDENT system, and all employees and contractors supporting its systems, have limited access based on their roles and need to know, and they are trained in the handling of personal information and PII for mission- and non-mission-related data (e.g., human capital and employment data). Training on specific systems will be conducted as appropriate. Annual refresher training is also provided on CD-ROM/DVD or online for existing employees and contractors. All DHS and US-VISIT system users must complete annual refresher training to retain system access.

8.3 What procedures are in place to determine which users may access the information and how does the project determine who has access?

US-VISIT has documented standard operating procedures to determine which users may access the IDENT system. The minimum requirements for access to the IDENT system are documented in the MOUs/data-sharing agreements between and among DHS and specific users, and in security, technical, and business documentation. In particular, individuals with system access must hold a DHS security clearance, must have a need to know the information based on their job responsibilities, and must participate in security and privacy training. Also data is filtered based on the User, so that one User that has access to IDENT may have access to more or less data than another User. The Data Provider decides who may have access to the data it provides.

Some contractors may have access to IDENT data. The extent of access will vary, based on the need to fulfill the requirements of the contract under appropriate nondisclosure and use limitations, in addition to requirements enumerated in section 8.1 of this document. US-VISIT ensures that all employees and contractors supporting its systems have limited access based on their roles and that they are trained in the handling of PII.

8.4 How does the project review and approve information sharing agreements, MOUs, new uses of the information, new access to the system by organizations within DHS and outside?

All MOUs must be reviewed and approved through an internal US-VISIT process, which includes a review by US-VISIT policy and privacy officials, and the DHS Office of the General Counsel. The US-VISIT approved MOU is sent to NPPD for review and concurrence, and is then forwarded to DHS for final review and approval by all DHS components.

Responsible Officials

Kenneth Gantt
Assistant Director
Program Integration and Mission Services Division
DHS/NPPD/US-VISIT

Approval Signature

Original signed and on file with the DHS Privacy Office

Jonathan R. Cantor
Acting Chief Privacy Officer
Department of Homeland Security

Appendix: A

Organization:

U.S. Department of State, Bureau of Consular Affairs (DoS/CA)

Purpose and Use:

The sharing between DoS/CA and US-VISIT supports the visa application and issuance process for aliens seeking to enter the United States.

DoS/CA consular officers working at DoS posts collect fingerprints from visa applicants and input them into the DoS Consular Consolidated Database (CCD) system. CCD is the DoS/CA gateway to IDENT.

DoS shares with US-VISIT biometrics, certain biographic data elements, and visa issuance or refusal data from visa applicants. US-VISIT then runs searches in the IDENT database and returns search results. DoS returns information regarding visa issuance or serious refusal of visas after a visa has been issued or denied.

Individuals Impacted:

The sharing between DoS/CA and US-VISIT impacts any individual who applies for a U.S. visa with DoS.

Data Elements:

DoS/CA searches and enrolls data it collects directly from visa applicants. The information returned from IDENT assists in determining identity and visa eligibility. IDENT also sends wrap-back notifications as described in the PIA overview. If visas are denied for a derogatory reason, DoS/CA transmits the relevant derogatory information for storage in IDENT. If visas are revoked for serious reasons, DoS/CA transmits the notice of revocation for storage in IDENT. These denial and revocation encounters are also added to the IDENT watchlist.

DoS/CA submits the following data elements:

Biometric data: finger scans and digital facial photographs

Encounter data: Place and date of issuance

Biographic data: name, date of birth, gender, physical details, and visa issuance or visa refusal data.

DoS/CA receives the following data elements from IDENT:

Biometric data: digital facial photograph

Biographic data: (1) full name (i.e., first, middle, last, nicknames, and aliases), date of birth, gender, signature; personal identifiers including Alien Registration Number, Social Security number (when provided), state identification number, civil record number, Federal Bureau of Investigation Fingerprint Number, Fingerprint Identification Number, National Unique Identification Number; and personal physical details, such as height, weight, eye color, and hair color; (2) identifiers for citizenship and nationality, including person-centric details, such as country of birth, country of citizenship, and nationality; (3) derogatory information,[27] if applicable, including wants and warrants, KSTs, sexual offender registration, and immigration violations; (4) IDENT watchlist status information; (5) miscellaneous officer comment information; (6) document information and identifiers (e.g., passport and visa data; document type; document number, and country of issuance); and (7) current and historic whereabouts.

Encounter data: transaction identifier data, such as sending organization; timestamp; workstation; reason fingerprinted, such as entry, visa application, credentialing application, or apprehension; and any available encounter information, including an IDENT-generated encounter identification number (EID).

Applicable IDENT SORN Routine Uses:

The sharing between DoS/CA and US-VISIT is authorized by Routine Use "H" of the IDENT SORN, which states that records may be disclosed to appropriate federal, state, local, tribal, foreign, or international agencies seeking information on the subjects of wants, warrants, or lookouts, or any other subject of interest for the specific purposes of administering or enforcing the law, national security, immigration, or intelligence, or carrying out DHS mission-related functions.

Partner Notice:

The DoS Consular Consolidated Database (CCD) PIA is available on the DoS website at http://www.state.gov/documents/organization/93772.pdf . The DoS Visa Records SORN, available at http://www.state.gov/documents/organization/102815.pdf, covers the data in CCD.

Retention by Partner:

DoS/CA retains all data received from IDENT.

Compliance Reporting:

Section 8 of the IDENT PIA covers US-VISIT compliance reporting. The MOU between DHS and DoS did not establish any additional compliance-reporting requirements.

Onward Transfer:

The DoS-DHS MOU limits access to DoS personnel who have a need to know to carry out their official duties and establishes that data may not be disseminated outside DoS without the expressed consent of DHS.

Training:

US-VISIT is currently developing an on-boarding package for distribution to all IDENT users. The package covers privacy compliance, as well as the relevant terms of any relevant MOU.

---

[27] A set of data related to negative or criminal information associated with an encounter.

Correction and Redress:

Legitimate travelers can submit concerns to and seek relief from DoS/CA regarding screening-related difficulties they may have experienced during travel to or from the United States by filing a complaint online at www.dhs.gov/trip and tracking their status using the control number assigned to the query. Redress is additionally available under the DoS Visa Records SORN, available at http://www.state.gov/documents/organization/102815.pdf.

Appendix: B

Organizations:

The Five Country Conference (FCC) is a forum for cooperation on migration and border security between the countries of Australia, Canada, New Zealand, the United Kingdom, and the United States (collectively called the FCC partners).

Purpose and Use:

The purpose of this information sharing is to support immigration processes, including asylum, visa, and refugee determinations, as well as admissibility, among the FCC partners. Foreign partners perform a search only; no data is enrolled in IDENT.

FCC countries use information shared through the FCC project for immigration and border management, national security, and law enforcement purposes in that country only.

FCC partners exchange their biometric data to search against the existing biometric holdings of other FCC partners to determine whether information pertinent to immigration and border management exists.

Individuals Impacted:

Individuals impacted include those encountered in the following immigration situations in an FCC partner country:

- Where there is an indication of derogatory activity (e.g., child smuggling) or other associations of concern such that the individual could be found inadmissible to one or more of the FCC partner countries.
- Where the identity of the individual is unknown (e.g., an individual who has destroyed his or her identifying documents or withheld information about his or her identity to prevent removal).
- Where there is reason to believe that another FCC partner has encountered the individual.
- Where there is an asylum claim that involves identifying individual(s) encountered inside the FCC partner country, or locating individuals whose whereabouts are unknown or who may have violated immigration or criminal laws.
- Where an individual requires re-documentation for removal or another immigration-related process.

Data Elements:

Shared information may include personal information relating to nationals of a FCC country that is deemed relevant and necessary for immigration or nationality determination purposes, as defined in the MOU. Shared information may include:

Biometric data: digital facial photographs and fingerprints.

Biographic data: full name, date of birth, place of birth, citizenship, document identifier (e.g., document type, document number, and country of issuance), current and historic whereabouts, gender, date fingerprinted, reason fingerprinted, location fingerprinted, and aliases.

In the event of an information match, two FCC partners (the requesting and providing countries) may further collaborate and review the match by exchanging additional information allowable under applicable law to determine whether further action is required using other existing protocols (law enforcement or otherwise) between the countries.

Applicable IDENT SORN Routine Uses:

Sharing among FCC partners is authorized by Routine Use "H" of the IDENT SORN, which states that records may be disclosed to appropriate federal, state, local, tribal, foreign, or international agencies seeking information on the subjects of wants, warrants, or lookouts, or any other subject of interest for the specific purposes of administering or enforcing the law, national security, immigration, or intelligence, or carrying out DHS mission-related functions.

Partner Notice:

The following FCC partner countries have provided notice by posting PIAs on this data exchange:

- Canada: http://www.cic.gc.ca/english/department/atip/pia-fcc.asp

- UK: http://www.ukba.homeoffice.gov.uk/sitecontent/documents/aboutus/workingwithus/high-value-data-sharing-protocol/pia.pdf?view=Binary.

- New Zealand: http://www.immigration.govt.nz/NR/rdonlyres/06901144-1618-4523-A5B9-340697315688/0/PrivacyImpactAssmt.pdf

- Australia: Australia conducts PIAs, but does not publicly post those documents.

Retention by Partner:

In general, all shared biometric information is destroyed securely as soon as the receiving country completes searching (whether or not a match is achieved). Shared biometric information is not used for any other purpose. When there is a legitimate purpose connected with a match and the information is still relevant, an FCC partner may store, process, and transmit further biometric and biographical information, in accordance with applicable laws and established information retention policies. When or if the case file includes shared information (either electronic or paper) for the individual to whom the data relates, that information may be retained as part of that case file in accordance with the domestic laws and data retention policies of the receiving country.

Compliance Reporting:

Any country may request assurance from another country that satisfactory safeguards are being maintained with respect to the information shared. This may include an audit of the safeguards, by an appropriate internal or external auditor with agreed terms of reference between the countries. The countries will also produce comprehensive, joint performance and management information about the operation of the protocol, which will explicitly identify the number and severity of any security or privacy breaches and remedial actions taken.

Onward Transfer:

Information received by any FCC partner is limited to use for determining the handling of an immigration case in that country only. FCC partners do not share information exchanged under this protocol with non-FCC partners without the permission of the FCC partner(s) that originally provided the information. For search requests resulting in matches against two or more countries, information may only be exchanged initially on a bilateral basis; however, the requesting country may inform each providing country about the existence of another matching record and the identity of the other FCC partner(s) with a matched record.

Training:

Privacy training for FCC partner participants complies with the appropriate training requirements defined by each FCC partner. All FCC Partner countries require that their employees complete Privacy and Security training.

Correction and Redress:

If an individual believes that the information held on him/her is incorrect, he or she may submit an inquiry to the following points of contact in each country;

Australia: DIAC, Minister for Immigration and Citizenship, Local Member of Parliament, Commonwealth Ombudsman or the Australian Privacy Commissioner.

New Zealand: A person may seek redress from one or all of the following: Immigration NZ, Minister of Immigration, Ombudsman or directly to the NZ Privacy Commissioner

UK: If the negative decision attracts a right of appeal, the appeal must be lodged with whichever part of U.K. Border Agency (UKBA) made the decision (for example, asylum for asylum cases, or the overseas visa hub for visa applications). If the person wants to simply know what information UKBA holds about them on its systems, they can make a request to the Subject Access Bureau at http://www.ukba.homeoffice.gov.uk/navigation/personal-data/

Canada: For access to personal information held by Citizenship and Immigration Canada please refer to their website at: http://www.cic.gc.ca/english/department/atip/requests-personal.asp.

Appendix: C

Organizations:

U.K. Border Agency (UKBA) International Group Visas Services Project (formerly known as UKvisas) and DHS (USCIS and US-VISIT).

Purpose and Use:

DHS will provide information to the UKBA International Group Services Project to help UKBA determine whether visa applicants for entry to the United Kingdom are eligible to obtain visas or other travel documents according to applicable U.K. laws.

The purpose of this information sharing is to assist UKBA in making visa or travel document determinations while supporting the DHS mission. This information sharing enables DHS to enhance the integrity of the U.S. immigration system by detecting, deterring, and pursuing immigration fraud, and to identify persons who pose a threat to national security and/or public safety. Although the DHS – UKBA MOU allows enrollment, the UKBA currently performs a search only; no data is enrolled in IDENT.

US-VISIT will use the biographic and biometric information received from the UKBA International Group Visa Services Project, and provided by the visa applicant, to determine whether the applicant's biometrics are currently included in the IDENT list of subjects of interest. In the event of a biometric match, US-VISIT will use additional biographic information provided by the United Kingdom to support any necessary law enforcement or immigration enforcement investigations.

Individuals Impacted:

This sharing impacts individuals applying for a U.K. visa from select locations, including the United States and Jamaica. The majority of those applying in the United States and Jamaica for a visa to enter the United Kingdom will be third-country nationals. However, U.S. citizens who intend to stay in the United Kingdom for longer than 3 months, or to enter the United Kingdom to engage in work, may also require a visa, according to U.K. immigration laws. Accordingly, U.S. persons may be included in data transfers between UKB and US-VISIT systems. As new locations are included in the project, those locations will be included in addenda to the DHS - UKBA MOU.

Data Elements:

Applicants submit their biographic information via the UKBA online visa application. Additionally, the applicant submits his or her biometric data (10 fingerprints and a digital facial photograph) at a USCIS ASC (which collects on behalf of UKBA) or a UKBA International Group Visa Services Project post. The following categories of information are required to complete the UKBA visa application:

Biometric data: digital facial photograph and 10 fingerprints

Biographic data: full name, date of birth, place of birth, country of citizenship, document identifier (e.g., document type, document number, and country of issuance), and gender.

The UKBA International Group Visa Service Project forwards the applicant's information, with the addition of a U.K. unique identification number, to US-VISIT. Only the 10 fingerprints will be queried against the IDENT list of subjects of interest. US-VISIT will not conduct name-based checks. If a match does *not* occur, US-VISIT will transmit two data elements back to the United Kingdom:

a) Status code: "None"

b) UK Unique Identifier.

US-VISIT will then delete all information pertaining to the applicant. If a match *does* occur, US-VISIT will transmit three data elements back to the United Kingdom:

a) Status code: "Watchlist"

b) UK Unique Identifier

c) Encounter ID.

The applicant's information may be stored in the Technical Reconciliation Analysis Classification System[28] (TRACS) for case management. In both cases (match or no-match), no information is stored in IDENT.

Applicable IDENT SORN Routine Uses:

This sharing between DHS and UKBA is authorized by Routine Use "H" of the IDENT SORN, which states that records may be disclosed to appropriate federal, state, local, tribal, foreign, or international agencies seeking information on the subjects of wants, warrants, or lookouts, or any other subject of interest for the specific purposes of administering or enforcing the law, national security, immigration, or intelligence, or carrying out DHS mission-related functions.

Partner Notice:

As the UKBA is not subject to the Privacy Act, it does not have a SORN covering its visa data. However, additional notice is provided by the UKBA International Group Visa Services website at www.ukvisas.gov.uk.

Retention by Partner:

The UKBA International Group Visa Services Project will retain the information provided by DHS until such time that UKBA has no mission-related need or after 75 years of its receipt from DHS, whichever is sooner. The 75-year retention period is necessary to support the holding of biometrics of subjects of interest in immigration and border management or law enforcement activities.

Compliance Reporting:

Section 8 of the IDENT PIA covers US-VISIT compliance reporting. The corresponding MOU for this project did not establish any additional compliance-reporting requirements.

---

[28] For a full discussion of TR ACS, see DHS/NPPD/USVISIT/PIA-004 Technical Reconciliation Analysis Classification System (TRACS), June 6, 2008

Onward Transfer:

The existing MOUs for this project do not outline any limitations.

Training:

The United Kingdom owns the biometric and biographic data of individuals who apply for visas and travel documents to the United Kingdom, and that nation provides privacy training to employees who access that data.

Correction and Redress:

The UKBA International Group Visa Services Project is solely responsible for granting or denying UKBA International Group Visa Services Project applications. The UKBA International Group Visa Services Project will determine whether any change to an applicant's information by US-VISIT, as a result of a successful redress request, will impact the adjudication process of the UKBA International Group Visa Services Project. The appeals process for handling inaccurate or erroneous information on behalf of the UKBA International Group Visa Services Project is solely the responsibility of the United Kingdom and can be found on the UKBA International Group Visa Services website at www.ukvisas.gov.uk.

If the applicant is denied a visa to enter the United Kingdom, the UKBA International Group Visa Services Project will provide a letter of visa denial and visa appeal to the applicant. The appeals process of the UKBA International Group Visa Services Project varies based on the circumstances upon which the applicant was denied a visa. The denial letter will detail the process the applicant must follow to appeal the visa decision. Individuals who are denied visas to enter the United Kingdom may refer to the UKBA website at http://www.ukba.homeoffice.gov.uk/visas-immigration/visiting/general/appeals/ for more information.

Appendix: D

Organization:

United States (U.S.) Department of Defense (DOD)

Purpose and Use:

Information sharing with DOD supports the missions of DOD and DHS. For DOD, relevant missions include active military operations, warfighter, detainee affairs, force protection efforts, anti-terrorism, special operations, stability operations, homeland defense, counterintelligence, and intelligence. For DHS, relevant missions include critical infrastructure protection, transportation and border security, law enforcement, administration of immigration benefits, emergency management, intelligence, and other interests of the United States.

Current biometric data sharing between DOD and the Office of Biometric Identity Management (OBIM) is mostly through manual processes. The Automated Biometric Identification System (ABIS) is DOD's multi-modal biometric system for matching, storing, and sharing biometrics in support of military operations with government agencies and with partner nations. The DOD Biometric Enabled Watchlist (BEWL) is located in ABIS. The National Ground Intelligence Center (NGIC) is responsible for adding persons to BEWL. The BEWL includes known or suspected terrorists, national security threats, and DOD detainees.[29] Those identities are subsequently transmitted to OBIM by DOD's Biometric Identity Management Agency (BIMA) through a secure file transfer protocol (SFTP) site. The biometric records are then enrolled in the DHS Automated Biometric Identification System (IDENT) and added to the IDENT watchlist, which is available to all DHS stakeholders searching IDENT. OBIM in turn provides information to DOD on matches in IDENT where permissible, on those enrolled records from the BEWL. OBIM checks IDENT for any subsequent encounters on these DOD BEWL records and shares this information with DOD, where permissible.

To support the DHS mission, DHS also receives DOD latent prints on a daily basis through the Federal Bureau of Investigation (FBI). All submissions to the FBI's Universal Latent File are also submitted for search against the entire IDENT gallery.

Going forward, OBIM and DOD recognize the need to increase biometric data sharing through an automated connection between IDENT and ABIS to create interoperability. Through IDENT-ABIS interoperability, DHS and DOD will directly link IDENT and ABIS to enable searches by end users of each system. Through IDENT-ABIS interoperability in the future, both DHS and DOD will have access to expanded datasets from the other system.

Individuals Impacted:

KSTs, national security threats, DOD detainees and individuals of interest to DOD and DHS. Information shared may contain information about U.S. Persons.

---

[29] Detainees are individuals who are detained by DOD for at least 2 weeks and are issued an internment serial number, but who have not been vetted by NGIC analysts for a formal threat determination.

Data Elements:

ABIS is DOD's authoritative, multi-modal biometric system for matching, storing, and sharing biometrics in support of military operations, with government agencies, and with partner nations.

ABIS encounter information could contain data elements such as: ABIS encounter specific identifier, reason fingerprinted, date fingerprinted, arrest segment literal, fingerprinting agency, fingerprints, iris images, facial images, palmprints, name, aliases, date of birth, place of birth, country of citizenship, and gender.

IDENT encounter information could contain data elements such as: digital facial photographs, fingerprints, IDENT unique identifiers, IDENT organization/unit/sub-unit, encounter information, encounter specific identifier, name, aliases, date of birth, place of birth, country of citizenship, nationality, gender, and date fingerprinted.

In the event of an information match, the partners may further collaborate and review the match by exchanging additional information allowable under applicable law to determine whether further action is required using other existing protocols (law enforcement or otherwise) between the countries.

Applicable IDENT SORN Routine Uses:

The sharing of PII outside of DHS is compatible with the original collection of that information and is covered by the IDENT SORN, 72 FR 31080 (June 5, 2007).

All or a part of the data contained in IDENT records may be disclosed as a routine use to appropriate federal, state, local, tribal, foreign, or international agencies seeking information on the subjects of wants, warrants, or lookouts, or any other subject of interest for the specific purposes of administering or enforcing the law, national security, immigration, or intelligence, or carrying out DHS mission-related functions as determined by DHS (Routine Use J).

Partner Notice:

This information is covered by two DOD SORNs: Defense Biometric Services, 74 Fed. Reg. 48237 (Sep. 22, 2009), available at http://dpclo.defense.gov/privacy/SORNS/dod/A0025-2_SAIS_DoD.html, and Department of Defense Detainee Biometric Information System, 72 Fed. Reg. 14534 (Mar. 28, 2007), available at http://dpclo.defense.gov/privacy/SORNs/dod/A0025-2c_SAIS_DoD.html.

Retention by Partner:

DHS and DOD will retain the data only as long as is needed to fulfill the purposes of the project. In no instance will the retention period of any data item exceed the maximum period permissible by applicable legal and regulatory requirements or official retention policies.

Compliance Reporting:

Both DHS and DOD may audit the access, use, handling, and maintenance of each other's data to ensure compliance. DHS and DOD may independently audit and inspect the other's use of data provided and review the audit records of the other agency. The agencies may also accept the results of internal agency audits (such as Inspector General audits) conducted in lieu of an audit.

Onward Transfer:

Both agencies acknowledge that data stored on behalf of third parties, or subsequent matches to that data, will not be shared without the consent of the data owner.

Where a Party receives a third party request for information shared under the MOA, such as a request under the Freedom of Information Act or the Privacy Act, or through Congressional or media request, or any other method, that Party will ensure that it does not adjudicate such requests for the other Party. The Party receiving a third party request for information which is owned or originated by the other Party shall immediately consult with the other Party as to how to respond to the request.

Training:

DOD personnel with access to data shared are trained in the protection and proper treatment of all data, to ensure overall safeguarding of the information, in accordance with the Privacy Act and other applicable laws and policies, including but not limited to confidentiality regulations associated with particular immigration benefits.

DOD abides by DHS' privacy policies, ensures that its employees, including contractors and detailees from third agencies with access to any of DHS' data, have completed any required privacy and information assurance training on the handling of all data.

DOD also trains designated users on techniques to effectively query any shared systems, if requested. The training will include an explanation of data fields and be closely coordinated by DHS.

Correction and Redress:

OBIM redress measures are discussed in Section 7 of the PIA.

Both agencies maintain an ability to locate and correct PII maintained by the other department. Additionally, DOD corrects any disseminated information based on the information that is later deemed to be erroneous. DOD must provide written confirmation to DHS of the corrections made. The applicable SORNs cited above provide instructions for submitting a redress request to DOD.

Appendix: E

Organizations:

The Governments of the United States of America and the Republic of Estonia.

Purpose and Use:

The purpose of the Preventing and Combating Serious Crime (PCSC) agreements is to enhance and expedite cooperation between the Parties in preventing and combating serious crime. The PCSC agreements are designed to facilitate the timely exchange of case specific information between the signatories regarding the prevention, detection, and investigation of serious criminal activities. Serious criminal activity excludes minor criminal offenses and generally may have the effect of rendering an individual inadmissible or removable from the United States. This includes inquiries at the border when an individual has been identified for further inspection.

PCSC agreements do not provide for bulk screening or bulk sharing of data. The Agreements enable the parties' national contact points to query individual fingerprint records through an automated system. In individual cases where there is a match and in compliance with the supplying country's national law, the supplying country may supply the requesting country further information to assist with law enforcement efforts in both countries. In certain cases, such as terrorism-related cases, with the foreign partner's permission data may be enrolled in IDENT. The PCSC agreement can facilitate near real-time law enforcement-to-law enforcement cooperation critical to the prevention and investigation of serious crime.

Individuals Impacted:

The government of the U.S.A. and the Republic of Estonia will share information on citizens and third party nationals who are suspected or convicted of committing serious crimes.

Data Elements:

Biometric data: digital facial photograph and fingerprints

Biographic data: Name (first and last, other), Date fingerprinted, Reason fingerprinted, Location fingerprinted, Aliases, Nationality, Place of Birth, Date of Birth, Gender, Travel and Identity document information, Encounter information (Transaction-identifier data includes the sending organization; timestamp; reason sent, such as entry, visa application, credentialing application, or apprehension; and any available encounter information).

In the event of an information match, the partners may further collaborate and review the match by exchanging additional information allowable under applicable law to determine whether further action is required using other existing protocols (law enforcement or otherwise) between the countries.

Applicable IDENT SORN Routine Uses:

This sharing of information from IDENT on matches on biometric queries from the Republic of Estonia is authorized by Routine Use "H" of the IDENT SORN, which states that records may be disclosed to appropriate federal, state, local, tribal, foreign, or international agencies seeking information on the subjects of wants, warrants, or lookouts, or any other subject of interest for the specific purposes of administering or enforcing the law, national security, immigration, or intelligence, or carrying out DHS mission-related functions.

For queries going out from DHS, this sharing is authorized by DHS/ICE-011 - Immigration Enforcement Operational Records System (ENFORCE), 75 Fed. Reg. 23274 (May 3, 2010); DHS/USVISIT-0004 - DHS Automated Biometric Identification System (IDENT), 72 Fed. Reg. 31080 (Jun. 5, 2007).

Partner Notice: Estonia provides public notice on the collection of personal information through the public website for legal acts (www.riigiteataja.ee) and also through the websites of the responsible authorities, as required by the Estonian Public Information Act of 2000 and the Estonian Personal Data Protection Act of 2008.

Retention by Partner:

If there is no match to the initial query, all transmitted biometric information is deleted. The receiving country is required to destroy the biometric information in a secure manner and use it for no other purpose once the search against its relevant biometric systems is complete. If there is a match in the receiving country's database, the supplying country will determine whether or not sharing further information on the subject is permissible under its national law. When there is a legitimate purpose connected with a match, either country may store, process, and transmit biometric and biographical information shared through a follow-up exchange, in accordance with applicable national laws and established information retention policies.

Compliance Reporting:

Under the Agreement, the Parties are required to maintain documentation, such as audit logs of the transmission and receipt of data communicated under the Agreement. This documentation, and the systems which collect and store the subject data, will be periodically evaluated to ensure compliance with the terms set forth in the Agreement, applicable Interface Control Documents, and any other implementing arrangements. The Parties have agreed to cooperate with each other on requests for such documentation records.

Onward Transfer:

The PCSC agreement does not permit the further communication of data provided under the Agreement to any third State, international body, or private entity without the consent of the country that provided the data and without the appropriate safeguards.

Training:

All system users receive basic training and also a follow up training as ongoing training needs and changes in legislation dictate.

Correction and Redress:

Individuals may request access to personal information through the Police and Border Guard Board or through the Ministry of Justice. Information requests can be filed by mail or email. Estonian residents (including foreign nationals who possess an Estonian residence permit) also have the option to access their personal information through the e-governance state portal (www.eesti.ee), which allows them to view a log of others who have accessed their data. Individuals may request correction to personal information pursuant to legislation, regulations and guidelines.

Police and Border Guard Board
Pärnu mnt 139, Tallinn 15060
+372-612-3000
E-mail: ppa@politsei.ee

Ministry of Justice
Tõnismägi 5a, Tallinn 15191
+372-620-8100
E-mail: info@just.ee

Appendix: F

Organizations:

The Governments of the United States of America and the Czech Republic

Purpose and Use:

The purpose of the Preventing and Combating Serious Crime (PCSC) agreements is to enhance and expedite cooperation between the Parties in preventing and combating serious crime. The PCSC agreements are designed to facilitate the timely exchange of case specific information between the signatories regarding the prevention, detection, and investigation of serious criminal activities. Serious criminal activity excludes minor criminal offences and generally may have the effect of rendering an individual inadmissible or removable from the United States. This includes inquiries at the border when an individual has been identified for further inspection.

PCSC agreements do not provide for bulk screening or bulk sharing of data. The Agreements enable the parties' national contact points to query individual fingerprint records through an automated system. In individual cases where there is a match and in compliance with the supplying country's national law, the supplying country may supply the requesting country further information to assist with law enforcement efforts in both countries. In certain cases, such as terrorism-related cases, with the foreign partner's permission data may be enrolled in IDENT. The PCSC agreement can facilitate near real-time law enforcement-to-law enforcement cooperation critical to the prevention and investigation of serious crime.

Individuals impacted

The governments of the U.S.A. and the Czech Republic will share information on citizens and third party nationals who are suspected or convicted of committing serious crimes.

Data Elements:

Biometric data: digital facial photograph and fingerprints

Biographic data: Name (first and last, other), Date fingerprinted, Reason fingerprinted, Location fingerprinted, Aliases, Nationality, Place of Birth, Date of Birth, Gender, Travel and Identity document information, Encounter information (Transaction-identifier data includes the sending organization; timestamp; reason sent, such as entry, visa application, credentialing application, or apprehension; and any available encounter information). Other information held in US-VISIT and ICE systems may also be exchanged.

In the event of an information match, the partners may further collaborate and review the match by exchanging additional information allowable under applicable law to determine whether further action is required using other existing protocols (law enforcement or otherwise) between the countries.

Applicable IDENT SORN Routine Uses:

This sharing of information from IDENT on matches on biometric queries from the Czech Republic is authorized by Routine Use "H" of the IDENT SORN, which states that records may be

disclosed to appropriate federal, state, local, tribal, foreign, or international agencies seeking information on the subjects of wants, warrants, or lookouts, or any other subject of interest for the specific purposes of administering or enforcing the law, national security, immigration, or intelligence, or carrying out DHS mission-related functions.

For queries going out from DHS, this sharing is authorized by DHS/ICE-011 - Immigration Enforcement Operational Records System (ENFORCE), 75 Fed. Reg. 23274 (May 3, 2010).

Partner Notice:

Public notice of the collection and processing of personal information in the Czech Republic is contained in law. According to Section 60 of the Act 273/2008 Coll., the Czech police is entitled to collect and process personal information to the extent necessary for performance of its tasks (which according to Section 2 of the same Act, include prevention of crime, along with protection of persons, property and public order). The Act also lists essential information on access of Police to various state or public databases and information systems, along with the powers of the police to collect and process personal data. Pursuant to Section 83 of this Act, any individual has right to ask about personal information that is processed by the police and to request correction, erasure, amendment, or blocking of incorrect or inaccurate personal data.

Retention by Partner:

If there is no match to the initial query, all transmitted biometric information is deleted. The receiving country is required to destroy the biometric information in a secure manner and use it for no other purpose once the search against its relevant biometric systems is complete. If there is a match in the receiving country's database, the supplying country will determine whether or not sharing further information on the subject is permissible under its national law. When there is a legitimate purpose connected with a match, either country may store, process, and transmit biometric and biographical information shared through a follow-up exchange, in accordance with applicable national laws and established information retention policies.

Compliance Reporting:

Under the Agreement, the Parties are required to maintain documentation, such as audit logs of the transmission and receipt of data communicated under the Agreement. This documentation, and the systems which collect and store the subject data, will be periodically evaluated to ensure compliance with the terms set forth in the Agreement, applicable Interface Control Documents, and any other implementing arrangements. The Parties have agreed to cooperate with each other on requests for such documentation records where permissible.

Onward Transfer:

The PCSC agreement does not permit the further communication of data provided under the Agreement to any third State, international body, or private entity without the consent of the country that provided the data and without the appropriate safeguards.

Training:

The Police Presidium's Personal Data Department trains and advises police personnel on processing of personal data. Aside from organizing periodic training sessions for police personnel on data privacy and handling procedures, the department also advises police personnel on handling of individual cases and supervises all data privacy programs within the Police Presidium.

Correction and Redress:

Written requests for access or redress can be sent to:

Police Presidium of the Czech Republic
Strojnická 27 (PO BOX 62/K-SOU)
170 89 Prague 7
Czech Republic

Requests may be also filed in person to any police station during public hours. The requests are free of charge. Follow-up or repeat requests can be filed six months after the original inquiry.

In order to process a request, the data subject must provide information necessary for identification (name and surname, date of birth, place of residence or address for correspondence). If a lawyer makes request on behalf of another person, a notarized power of attorney must be enclosed. Otherwise, the signatures on a request will have to be verified in person.

Replies are sent within 60 days by certified mail.

Appendix: G

Organizations:

The Governments of the United States of America and the Slovak Republic

Purpose and Use:

The purpose of the Preventing and Combating Serious Crime (PCSC) agreements is to enhance and expedite cooperation between the Parties in preventing and combating serious crime. The PCSC agreements are designed to facilitate the timely exchange of case specific information between the signatories regarding the prevention, detection, and investigation of serious criminal activities. Serious criminal activity excludes minor criminal offences and generally may have the effect of rendering an individual inadmissible or removable from the United States. This includes inquiries at the border when an individual has been identified for further inspection.

PCSC agreements do not provide for bulk screening or bulk sharing of data. The Agreements enable the parties' national contact points to query individual fingerprint records through an automated system. In individual cases where there is a match and in compliance with the supplying country's national law, the supplying country may supply the requesting country further information to assist with law enforcement efforts in both countries. In certain cases, for example terrorism related cases, with the foreign partner's permission data may be enrolled in IDENT. The PCSC agreement can facilitate near real-time law enforcement-to-law enforcement cooperation critical to the prevention and investigation of serious crime.

Individuals impacted

The governments of the U.S.A. and the Slovak Republic will share information on citizens and third party nationals who are suspected or convicted of committing serious crimes.

Data Elements:

Biometric data: digital facial photograph and fingerprints

Biographic data: Name (first and last, other), Date fingerprinted, Reason fingerprinted, Location fingerprinted, Aliases, Nationality, Place of Birth, Date of Birth, Gender, Travel and Identity document information, Encounter information (Transaction-identifier data includes the sending organization; timestamp; reason sent, such as entry, visa application, credentialing application, or apprehension; and any available encounter information).

In the event of an information match, the partners may further collaborate and review the match by exchanging additional information allowable under applicable law to determine whether further action is required using other existing protocols (law enforcement or otherwise) between the countries.

Applicable IDENT SORN Routine Uses:

This sharing of information from IDENT on matches on biometric queries from the Slovak Republic is authorized by Routine Use "H" of the IDENT SORN, which states that records may be disclosed to appropriate federal, state, local, tribal, foreign, or international agencies seeking information on the subjects of wants, warrants, or lookouts, or any other subject of interest for the specific purposes of administering or enforcing the law, national security, immigration, or intelligence, or carrying out DHS mission-related functions.

For queries going out from DHS, this sharing is authorized by DHS/ICE-011 - Immigration Enforcement Operational Records System (ENFORCE), 75 Fed. Reg. 23274 (May 3, 2010).

Partner Notice:

Sections 69 through 69g of Act No. 171/1993 Coll. on the Police Force provide notice about the processing of personal data by the Police Force.

Retention by Partner:

If there is no match to the initial query, all transmitted biometric information is deleted. The receiving country is required to destroy the biometric information in a secure manner and use it for no other purpose once the search against its relevant biometric systems is complete. If there is a match in the receiving country's database, the supplying country will determine whether or not sharing further information on the subject is permissible under its national law. When there is a legitimate purpose connected with a match, either country may store, process, and transmit biometric and biographical information shared through a follow-up exchange, in accordance with applicable national laws and established information retention policies.

Compliance Reporting:

Under the Agreement, the Parties are required to maintain documentation, such as audit logs of the transmission and receipt of data communicated under the Agreement. This documentation, and the systems which collect and store the subject data, will be periodically evaluated to ensure compliance with the terms set forth in the Agreement, applicable Interface Control Documents, and any other implementing arrangements. The Parties have agreed to cooperate with each other on requests for such documentation records where permissible.

Onward Transfer:

The PCSC agreement does not permit the further communication of data provided under the Agreement to any third State, international body, or private entity without the consent of the country that provided the data and without the appropriate safeguards.

Training:

All police officers who process personal data while carrying out service tasks are required to take special training on international agreements as well as Acts of the Slovak Republic and internal regulations of the Police Force, which contain provisions relevant to data protection and processing of personal data.

Correction and Redress:

Written requests for access and correction of personal data can be sent to:

Ministry of Interior of the Slovak Republic

Pribinova 2
812 72 Bratislava
skis@minv.sk

The Police Force must respond to the applicant no later than 30 days from the receipt of the request. The request is free of charge.

Appendix: H

Organizations:

The Governments of the United States of America and the Kingdom of Spain

Purpose and Use:

The purpose of the Preventing and Combating Serious Crime (PCSC) agreements is to enhance and expedite cooperation between the Parties in preventing and combating serious crime. The PCSC agreements are designed to facilitate the timely exchange of case specific information between the signatories regarding the prevention, detection, and investigation of serious criminal activities. Serious criminal activity excludes minor criminal offenses and generally may have the effect of rendering an individual inadmissible or removable from the United States. This includes inquiries at the border when an individual has been identified for further inspection.

PCSC agreements do not provide for bulk screening or bulk sharing of data. The Agreements enable the parties' national contact points to query individual fingerprint records through an automated system. In individual cases where there is a match and in compliance with the supplying country's national law, the supplying country may supply the requesting country further information to assist with law enforcement efforts in both countries. In certain cases, for example terrorism related cases, with the foreign partner's permission data may be enrolled in IDENT. The PCSC agreement can facilitate near real-time law enforcement-to-law enforcement cooperation critical to the prevention and investigation of serious crime.

Individuals Impacted:

The governments of the U.S.A. and the Kingdom of Spain will share information on citizens and third party nationals who are suspected or convicted of committing serious crimes. **Data Elements**:

Biometric data: digital facial photograph and fingerprints

Biographic data: Name (first and last, other), Date fingerprinted, Reason fingerprinted, Location fingerprinted, Aliases, Nationality, Place of Birth, Date of Birth, Gender, Travel and Identity document information, Encounter information (Transaction-identifier data includes the sending organization; timestamp; reason sent, such as entry, visa application, credentialing application, or apprehension; and any available encounter information).

In the event of an information match, the partners may further collaborate and review the match by exchanging additional information allowable under applicable law to determine whether further action is required using other existing protocols (law enforcement or otherwise) between the countries.

Applicable IDENT SORN Routine Uses:

This sharing of information from IDENT on matches on biometric queries from the Republic of Estonia is authorized by Routine Use "H" of the IDENT SORN, which states that records may be disclosed to appropriate federal, state, local, tribal, foreign, or international agencies seeking information on the subjects of wants, warrants, or lookouts, or any other subject of interest for the specific purposes of administering or enforcing the law, national security, immigration, or intelligence, or carrying out DHS mission-related functions.

For queries going out from DHS, this sharing is authorized by DHS/ICE-011 - Immigration Enforcement Operational Records System (ENFORCE), 75 Fed. Reg. 23274 (May 3, 2010).

Partner Notice:

The Spanish Personal Data Protection Law of 1999 in its Article 5 gives notice to individuals as to how personal data will be collected, treated, handled and stored.

Retention by Partner:

If there is no match to the initial query, all transmitted biometric information is deleted. The receiving country is required to destroy the biometric information in a secure manner and use it for no other purpose once the search against its relevant biometric systems is complete. If there is a match in the receiving country's database, the supplying country will determine whether or not sharing further information on the subject is permissible under its national law. When there is a legitimate purpose connected with a match, either country may store, process, and transmit biometric and biographical information shared through a follow-up exchange, in accordance with applicable national laws and established information retention policies.

Compliance Reporting:

Under the Agreement, the Parties are required to maintain documentation, such as audit logs of the transmission and receipt of data communicated under the Agreement. This documentation, and the systems which collect and store the subject data, will be periodically evaluated to ensure compliance with the terms set forth in the Agreement, applicable Interface Control Documents, and any other implementing arrangements. The Parties have agreed to cooperate with each other on requests for such documentation records.

Onward Transfer:

The PCSC agreement does not permit the further communication of data provided under the Agreement to any third State, international body, or private entity without the consent of the country that provided the data and without the appropriate safeguards.

Training:

The Spanish Data Protection Agency trains and monitors on a continuous basis all the agents involved in the collection and handling of personal data as mandated by Article 37 (f) of Spanish Personal Data Protection Law of 1999.

Correction and Redress:

Individuals can request access to their own personal information under the Spanish Personal Data Protection law by requesting it to the Spanish Data Protection Agency - Subdirectorate for the Inspection of the Data Protection Agency. The request for access of personal information has to be sent in writing to:

Subdirección General de Inspección de Datos

Agencia Española de Protección de Datos
Calle Jorge Juan, 6-28001-Madrid
Or by fax to +34 914 455 699

The POC for redress if the breach was caused by Government:

Spanish Data Protection Agency
Subdireccion General de Inspeccion
Calle Jorge Juan 6
Madrid 28001
Or by fax +34 914 455 699

Appendix: I

Organizations:

The Governments of United States of America and the Principality of Andorra

Purpose and Use:

The purpose of the Preventing and Combating Serious Crime (PCSC) agreements is to enhance and expedite cooperation between the Parties in preventing and combating serious crime. The PCSC agreements are designed to facilitate the timely exchange of case specific information between the signatories regarding the prevention, detection, and investigation of serious criminal activities. Serious criminal activity excludes minor criminal offenses and generally may have the effect of rendering an individual inadmissible or removable from the United States. This includes inquiries at the border when an individual has been identified for further inspection.

PCSC agreements do not provide for bulk screening or bulk sharing of data. The Agreements enable the parties' national contact points to query individual fingerprint records through an automated system. In individual cases where there is a match and in compliance with the supplying country's national law, the supplying country may supply the requesting country further information to assist with law enforcement efforts in both countries. In certain cases, for example terrorism related cases, with the foreign partner's permission data may be enrolled in IDENT. The PCSC agreement can facilitate near real-time law enforcement-to-law enforcement cooperation critical to the prevention and investigation of serious crime.

Individuals Impacted:

Information will be shared on individuals that are suspected or convicted of committing serious crimes. In addition to third party nationals, this can include citizens of both the United States and the Principality of Andorra.

Data Elements:

Biometric data: digital facial photograph and fingerprints

Biographic data: Data exchanged under this project may include (but not limited to):

Name (first and last, other), Date fingerprinted, Reason fingerprinted, Location fingerprinted, Aliases, Nationality, Place of Birth, Date of Birth, Gender, Travel and Identity document information, Encounter information (Transaction-identifier data includes the sending organization; timestamp; reason sent, such as entry, visa application, credentialing application, or apprehension; and any available encounter information).

In the event of an information match, the partners may further collaborate and review the match by exchanging additional information allowable under applicable law to determine whether further action is required using other existing protocols (law enforcement or otherwise) between the countries.

Applicable IDENT SORN Routine Uses:

This sharing of information from IDENT on matches on biometric queries from the Principality of Andorra is authorized by Routine Use "H" of the IDENT SORN, which states that records may be

disclosed to appropriate federal, state, local, tribal, foreign, or international agencies seeking information on the subjects of wants, warrants, or lookouts, or any other subject of interest for the specific purposes of administering or enforcing the law, national security, immigration, or intelligence, or carrying out DHS mission-related functions.

For queries going out from DHS, this sharing is authorized by DHS/ICE-011 - Immigration Enforcement Operational Records System (ENFORCE) May 3, 2010, 75 FR 23274.

Partner Notice:

According to the Law 15/2003, of 18th December, on personal data protection, the creation, rectification and erasure of public files has to be regulated by a decree published in the Official Journal of the Principality of Andorra unless otherwise regulated by a specific Law.

Files with private purposes must be registered before its creation by the controller of the data in the public registry run by the supervisory authority: the Andorran Data Protection Agency (ADPA). Privacy notices for private organizations are available on the APDA website. Privacy notices for public organizations are published in the Official Gazette.

Retention by Partner:

If there is no match to the initial query, all transmitted biometric information is deleted. The receiving country is required to destroy the biometric information in a secure manner and use it for no other purpose once the search against its relevant biometric systems is complete. If there is a match in the receiving country's database, the supplying country will determine whether or not sharing further information on the subject is permissible under its national law. When there is a legitimate purpose connected with a match, either country may store, process, and transmit biometric and biographical information shared through a follow-up exchange, in accordance with applicable national laws and established information retention policies.

Compliance Reporting:

Under the Agreement, the Parties are required to maintain documentation, such as audit logs of the transmission and receipt of data communicated under the Agreement. This documentation, and the systems which collect and store the subject data, will be periodically evaluated to ensure compliance with the terms set forth in the Agreement, applicable Interface Control Documents, and any other implementing arrangements. The Parties have agreed to cooperate with each other on requests for such documentation records.

Onward Transfer:

The PCSC agreement does not permit the further communication of data provided under the Agreement to any third State, international body, or private entity without the consent of the country that provided the data and without the appropriate safeguards.

Training:

The ADPA publishes two *Good practice manuals* with tips on how to use and handle personal information properly. One of these is specifically addressed to officials who handle personal information.

The manuals are on the Agency's website, https://www.apda.ad/. All Andorran Police officials who handle personal information are trained via the manual.

Correction and Redress:

Individuals may request access to personal information by writing to:

Andorran Police (Cos de Policia d'Andorra)
Despatx Central de Policia, Ed. Administratiu de l'Obac, Crta. de l'Obac s/n,
Escaldes-Engordany
Andorra
Tel: (+376) 872 000
Fax: (+376) 872 004
policia@andorra.ad

Individuals may request correction of personal data by writing to:

Andorran Police (Cos de Policia d'Andorra)
Despatx Central de Policia, Ed. Administratiu de l'Obac, Crta. de l'Obac s/n,
Escaldes-Engordany
Andorra
Tel: (+376) 872 000
Fax: (+376) 872 004
policia@andorra.ad

For any issues or concerns regarding proper handling of personal information, access or redress, please contact the Andorran Data Protection Agency.

Andorran Data Protection Agency (L'Agència Andorrana de Protecció de Dades)
Carrer Dr. Vilanova núm. 15, planta -5
Andorra la Vella
Telèfon: (+376) 808 115
Fax: (+376) 808 118
https://www.apda.ad/contact/

Appendix: J

Organizations:

The Governments of United States of America and the Portuguese Republic

Purpose and Use:

The purpose of the Preventing and Combating Serious Crime (PCSC) agreements is to enhance and expedite cooperation between the Parties in preventing and combating serious crime. The PCSC agreements are designed to facilitate the timely exchange of case specific information between the signatories regarding the prevention, detection, and investigation of serious criminal activities. Serious criminal activity excludes minor criminal offenses and generally may have the effect of rendering an individual inadmissible or removable from the United States. This includes inquiries at the border when an individual has been identified for further inspection.

PCSC agreements do not provide for bulk screening or bulk sharing of data. The Agreements enable the parties' national contact points to query individual fingerprint records through an automated system. In individual cases where there is a match and in compliance with the supplying country's national law, the supplying country may supply the requesting country further information to assist with law enforcement efforts in both countries. In certain cases, for example terrorism related cases, with the foreign partner's permission data may be enrolled in IDENT. The PCSC agreement can facilitate near real-time law enforcement-to-law enforcement cooperation critical to the prevention and investigation of serious crime.

Individuals Impacted:

Information will be shared on individuals that are suspected or convicted of committing serious crimes. In addition to third party nationals, this can include citizens of both the United States and the Portuguese Republic.

Data Elements:

Biometric data: digital facial photograph and fingerprints

Biographic data: Data exchanged under this project may include (but not limited to):

Name (first and last, other), Date fingerprinted, Reason fingerprinted, Location fingerprinted, Aliases, Nationality, Place of Birth, Date of Birth, Gender, Travel and Identity document information, Encounter information (Transaction-identifier data includes the sending organization; timestamp; reason sent, such as entry, visa application, credentialing application, or apprehension; and any available encounter information).

In the event of an information match, the partners may further collaborate and review the match by exchanging additional information allowable under applicable law to determine whether further action is required using other existing protocols (law enforcement or otherwise) between the countries.

Applicable IDENT SORN Routine Uses:

This sharing of information from IDENT on matches on biometric queries from the Portuguese Republic is authorized by Routine Use "H" of the IDENT SORN, which states that records may be disclosed to appropriate federal, state, local, tribal, foreign, or international agencies seeking information on the subjects of wants, warrants, or lookouts, or any other subject of interest for the specific purposes of administering or enforcing the law, national security, immigration, or intelligence, or carrying out DHS mission-related functions.

For queries going out from DHS, this sharing is authorized by DHS/ICE-011 - Immigration Enforcement Operational Records System (ENFORCE) May 3, 2010, 75 FR 23274.

Partner Notice:

Portugal provides public notice on the collection of personal information through regulation published at the Official Journal (Lei 67/98; Lei 5/2008 and Deliberação 3191/2008).

Retention by Partner:

If there is no match to the initial query, all transmitted biometric information is deleted. The receiving country is required to destroy the biometric information in a secure manner and use it for no other purpose once the search against its relevant biometric systems is complete. If there is a match in the receiving country's database, the supplying country will determine whether or not sharing further information on the subject is permissible under its national law. When there is a legitimate purpose connected with a match, either country may store, process, and transmit biometric and biographical information shared through a follow-up exchange, in accordance with applicable national laws and established information retention policies.

Compliance Reporting:

Under the Agreement, the Parties are required to maintain documentation, such as audit logs of the transmission and receipt of data communicated under the Agreement. This documentation, and the systems which collect and store the subject data, will be periodically evaluated to ensure compliance with the terms set forth in the Agreement, applicable Interface Control Documents, and any other implementing arrangements. The Parties have agreed to cooperate with each other on requests for such documentation records.

Onward Transfer:

The PCSC agreement does not permit the further communication of data provided under the Agreement to any third State, international body, or private entity without the consent of the country that provided the data and without the appropriate safeguards.

Training:

Portugal: provides training to all authorized systems users according to their roles, including training in the handling of personal information and organizes meeting to discuss practical questions.

Correction and Redress:

For access and redress requests, contact:

Instituto Nacional de Medicina Legal e Ciências Forenses, I.P.
Largo da Sé Nova
3000-213 Coimbra
Tel.: (+351) 239 854 220
Fax: (+351) 239 836 470

and

Laboratório de Polícia Científica da Polícia Judiciária
Rua Gomes Freire, 174
1169-007 Lisboa
Tel: (+351) 218 641 587
Fax: (+351) 213 570 161
e-mail: lpc.sij@pj.pt

Appendix: K

Organizations:

The Governments of United States of America and the Republic of Malta

Purpose and Use:

The purpose of the Preventing and Combating Serious Crime (PCSC) agreements is to enhance and expedite cooperation between the Parties in preventing and combating serious crime. The PCSC agreements are designed to facilitate the timely exchange of case specific information between the signatories regarding the prevention, detection, and investigation of serious criminal activities. Serious criminal activity excludes minor criminal offenses and generally may have the effect of rendering an individual inadmissible or removable from the United States. This includes inquiries at the border when an individual has been identified for further inspection.

PCSC agreements do not provide for bulk screening or bulk sharing of data. The Agreements enable the parties' national contact points to query individual fingerprint records through an automated system. In individual cases where there is a match and in compliance with the supplying country's national law, the supplying country may supply the requesting country further information to assist with law enforcement efforts in both countries. In certain cases, for example terrorism related cases, with the foreign partner's permission data may be enrolled in IDENT. The PCSC agreement can facilitate near real-time law enforcement-to-law enforcement cooperation critical to the prevention and investigation of serious crime.

Individuals Impacted:

Information will be shared on individuals that are suspected or convicted of committing serious crimes. In addition to third party nationals, this can include citizens of both the United States and the Republic of Malta.

Data Elements:

Biometric data: digital facial photograph and fingerprints.

Biographic data: Data exchanged under this project may include (but not limited to): Name (first and last, other), Date fingerprinted, Reason fingerprinted, Location fingerprinted, Aliases, Nationality, Place of Birth, Date of Birth, Gender, Travel and Identity document information, Encounter information (Transaction-identifier data includes the sending organization; timestamp; reason sent, such as entry, visa application, credentialing application, or apprehension; and any available encounter information).

In the event of an information match, the partners may further collaborate and review the match by exchanging additional information allowable under applicable law to determine whether further action is required using other existing protocols (law enforcement or otherwise) between the countries.

Applicable IDENT SORN Routine Uses:

This sharing of information from IDENT on matches on biometric queries from the Republic of Malta is authorized by Routine Use "A" of the IDENT SORN, which states that records may be disclosed to appropriate federal, state, local, tribal, foreign, or international agencies seeking information on the subjects of wants, warrants, or lookouts, or any other subject of interest for the specific purposes of administering or enforcing the law, national security, immigration, or intelligence, or carrying out DHS mission-related functions.

For queries going out from DHS, this sharing is authorized by DHS/ICE-011 - Immigration Enforcement Operational Records System (ENFORCE) May 3, 2010, 75 FR 23274.

Partner Notice:

The Republic of Malta provides notice to individuals on an individual basis through a subject access request as provided in the Data Protection Act.

Retention by Partner:

If there is no match to the initial query, all transmitted biometric information is deleted. The receiving country is required to destroy the biometric information in a secure manner and use it for no other purpose once the search against its relevant biometric systems is complete. If there is a match in the receiving country's database, the supplying country will determine whether or not sharing further information on the subject is permissible under its national law. When there is a legitimate purpose connected with a match, either country may store, process, and transmit biometric and biographical information shared through a follow-up exchange, in accordance with applicable national laws and established information retention policies.

Compliance Reporting:

Under the Agreement, the Parties are required to maintain documentation, such as audit logs of the transmission and receipt of data communicated under the Agreement. This documentation, and the systems which collect and store the subject data, will be periodically evaluated to ensure compliance with the terms set forth in the Agreement, applicable Interface Control Documents, and any other implementing arrangements. The Parties have agreed to cooperate with each other on requests for such documentation records.

Onward Transfer:

The PCSC agreement does not permit the further communication of data provided under the Agreement to any third State, international body, or private entity without the consent of the country that provided the data and without the appropriate safeguards.

Training:

The Republic of Malta provides regular basic training on the handling of personal data and data protection matters to all serving members of the force at various levels. The regular basis of these trainings ensure timely updates to these officers with respect to legislative amendments and/or practical arrangements

Correction and Redress:

For Access:

Any individual may make a subject access request to check about the processing of his/her personal data to the Malta Police Data Protection officer. The contact details are:

Data Protection Office
Police General Headquarters
Floriana
Tel.No. +35622942196
Email:sandro.camilleri@gov.mt

For Redress:

Individuals may request correction to personal information by submitting a request to the Malta Police Data Protection Officer and they may also appeal within thirty days from the decision of the Malta Police Data Protection Officer to the Information and Data Protection Commissioner on the following contact details:

Office of the Information and Data Protection Commissioner
Airways House, Second Floor
High Street
Sliema SLM 1549
MALTA.
Tel: (+356) 2328 7100
Fax: (+356) 23287198
Email: idpc.info@gov.mt

Appendix: L

Organizations:

The Governments of United States of America and Hungary

Purpose and Use:

The purpose of the Preventing and Combating Serious Crime (PCSC) agreements is to enhance and expedite cooperation between the Parties in preventing and combating serious crime. The PCSC agreements are designed to facilitate the timely exchange of case specific information between the signatories regarding the prevention, detection, and investigation of serious criminal activities. Serious criminal activity excludes minor criminal offenses and generally may have the effect of rendering an individual inadmissible or removable from the United States. This includes inquiries at the border when an individual has been identified for further inspection.

PCSC agreements do not provide for bulk screening or bulk sharing of data. The Agreements enable the parties' national contact points to query individual fingerprint records through an automated system. In individual cases where there is a match and in compliance with the supplying country's national law, the supplying country may supply the requesting country further information to assist with law enforcement efforts in both countries. In certain cases, for example terrorism related cases, with the foreign partner's permission data may be enrolled in IDENT. The PCSC agreement can facilitate near real-time law enforcement-to-law enforcement cooperation critical to the prevention and investigation of serious crime.

Individuals Impacted:

Information will be shared on individuals that are suspected or convicted of committing serious crimes. In addition to third party nationals, this can include citizens of both the United States and Hungary.

Data Elements:

Biometric data: digital facial photograph and fingerprints

Biographic data: Data exchanged under this project may include (but not limited to):

Name (first and last, other), Date fingerprinted, Reason fingerprinted, Location fingerprinted, Aliases, Nationality, Place of Birth, Date of Birth, Gender, Travel and Identity document information, Encounter information (Transaction-identifier data includes the sending organization; timestamp; reason sent, such as entry, visa application, credentialing application, or apprehension; and any available encounter information).

In the event of an information match, the partners may further collaborate and review the match by exchanging additional information allowable under applicable law to determine whether further action is required using other existing protocols (law enforcement or otherwise) between the countries.

Applicable IDENT SORN Routine Uses:

This sharing of information from IDENT on matches on biometric queries from Hungary is authorized by Routine Use "A" of the IDENT SORN, which states that records may be disclosed to appropriate federal, state, local, tribal, foreign, or international agencies seeking information on the subjects of wants, warrants, or lookouts, or any other subject of interest for the specific purposes of administering or enforcing the law, national security, immigration, or intelligence, or carrying out DHS mission-related functions.

For queries going out from DHS, this sharing is authorized by DHS/ICE-011 - Immigration Enforcement Operational Records System (ENFORCE) May 3, 2010, 75 FR 23274.

Partner Notice:

Hungary provides public notice to the data subjects on the collection of personal information according to Act CXII of 2011 (On Informational Self-determination and Freedom of Information).

Retention by Partner:

If there is no match to the initial query, all transmitted biometric information is deleted. The receiving country is required to destroy the biometric information in a secure manner and use it for no other purpose once the search against its relevant biometric systems is complete. If there is a match in the receiving country's database, the supplying country will determine whether or not sharing further information on the subject is permissible under its national law. When there is a legitimate purpose connected with a match, either country may store, process, and transmit biometric and biographical information shared through a follow-up exchange, in accordance with applicable national laws and established information retention policies.

Compliance Reporting:

Under the Agreement, the Parties are required to maintain documentation, such as audit logs of the transmission and receipt of data communicated under the Agreement. This documentation, and the systems which collect and store the subject data, will be periodically evaluated to ensure compliance with the terms set forth in the Agreement, applicable Interface Control Documents, and any other implementing arrangements. The Parties have agreed to cooperate with each other on requests for such documentation records.

Onward Transfer:

The PCSC agreement does not permit the further communication of data provided under the Agreement to any third State, international body, or private entity without the consent of the country that provided the data and without the appropriate safeguards.

Training:

According to Hungarian data protection legislation, at any entity that deals with personal data, new employees receive a general training that includes the rules to be adhered to when dealing with databases of personal data. In case of changes as regards regulations of data protection, employees receive a follow-up training focusing on changes.

Correction and Redress:

For access:

The Hungarian National Authority for Data Protection and Freedom of Information in accordance with Section 66 of Act CXII of 2011 registers data processing undertaken in respect to personal data in a data protection file or registry in order to facilitate access to information for the data subject. The registry is public, the data subjects can for the moment obtain information on request, but the whole registry will be soon available and searchable on the authority's website (http://www.naih.hu/).

For redress:

After consulting the public registry, the data subject may turn to the data controller and in accordance of the Section 14 of the Privacy Act may request the following from the controller:

a. information on the control of personal data,

b. correction of personal data, and

c. deletion, blocking of personal data, with the exception of mandatory control.

In cases where the data subjects deem that the answer given by the data controller is inappropriate or the denial for giving him/her information was unlawful he/she may turn to the National Authority for Data Protection and Freedom of Information (NAIH) for redress.

H-1125 Budapest, Szilágyi Erzsébet fasor 22/C.
Telefon: +36 -1-391-1400
Fax: +36-1-391-1410
E-mail: privacy@naih.hu, web: www.naih.hu

Appendix: M

Organizations:

The Governments of United States of America and Commonwealth of Australia

Purpose and Use:

The purpose of the Preventing and Combating Serious Crime (PCSC) agreements is to enhance and expedite cooperation between the Parties in preventing and combating serious crime. The PCSC agreements are designed to facilitate the timely exchange of case specific information between the signatories regarding the prevention, detection, and investigation of serious criminal activities. Serious criminal activity excludes minor criminal offenses and generally has the effect of rendering an individual inadmissible or removable from the United States. This includes inquiries at the border when an individual has been identified for further inspection.

PCSC agreements do not provide for bulk screening or bulk sharing of data. The Agreements enable the parties' national contact points to query individual fingerprint records through an automated system. In individual cases where there is a match and in compliance with the supplying country's national law, the supplying country may supply the requesting country further information to assist with law enforcement efforts in both countries. In certain cases, for example terrorism related cases, with the foreign partner's permission data may be enrolled in IDENT. The PCSC agreement can facilitate near real-time law enforcement-to-law enforcement cooperation critical to the prevention and investigation of serious crime.

Individuals Impacted:

Information will be shared on individuals that are suspected or convicted of committing serious crimes. In addition to third party nationals, this can include citizens of both the United States and the Commonwealth of Australia.

Data Elements:

Biometric data: digital facial photograph and fingerprints.

Biographic data: Data exchanged under this project may include (but not limited to): Name (first and last, other), Date fingerprinted, Reason fingerprinted, Location fingerprinted, Aliases, Nationality, Place of Birth, Date of Birth, Gender, Travel and Identity document information, Encounter information (Transaction-identifier data includes the sending organization; timestamp; reason sent, such as entry, visa application, credentialing application, or apprehension; and any available encounter information).

In the event of an information match, the partners may further collaborate and review the match by exchanging additional information allowable under applicable law to determine whether further action is required using other existing protocols (law enforcement or otherwise) between the countries.

Applicable IDENT SORN Routine Uses:

This sharing of information from IDENT on matches on biometric queries from the Commonwealth of Australia is authorized by Routine Use "A" of the IDENT SORN, which states that records may be disclosed to appropriate federal, state, local, tribal, foreign, or international agencies seeking information on the subjects of wants, warrants, or lookouts, or any other subject of interest for the specific purposes of administering or enforcing the law, national security, immigration, or intelligence, or carrying out DHS mission-related functions.

For queries going out from DHS, this sharing is authorized by DHS/ICE-011 - Immigration Enforcement Operational Records System (ENFORCE) May 3, 2010, 75 FR 23274.

Partner Notice:

Australia provides public notice on the collection of personal information through the Personal Information Digest (PID) published in accordance with the *Privacy Act 1988*. The PID is available through the Office of the Australian Information Commission (OAIC) website http://www.oaic.gov.au.

Retention by Partner:

If there is no match to the initial query, all transmitted biometric information is deleted. The receiving country is required to destroy the biometric information in a secure manner and use it for no other purpose once the search against its relevant biometric systems is complete. If there is a match in the receiving country's database, the supplying country will determine whether or not sharing further information on the subject is permissible under its national law. When there is a legitimate purpose connected with a match, either country may store, process, and transmit biometric and biographical information shared through a follow-up exchange, in accordance with applicable national laws and established information retention policies.

Compliance Reporting:

Under the Agreement, the Parties are required to maintain documentation, such as audit logs of the transmission and receipt of data communicated under the Agreement. This documentation, and the systems which collect and store the subject data, will be periodically evaluated to ensure compliance with the terms set forth in the Agreement, applicable Interface Control Documents, and any other implementing arrangements. The Parties have agreed to cooperate with each other on requests for such documentation records.

Onward Transfer:

The PCSC agreement does not permit the further communication of data provided under the Agreement to any third State, international body, or private entity without the consent of the country that provided the data and without the appropriate safeguards.

Training:

Australia provides training to authorized system users in accordance with their roles, procedures and on basic application of relevant legislation.

Correction and Redress:

Individuals may request access to personal information under the Privacy Act through the Freedom of Information Act.

The Australian Federal Police

Freedom of Information contact officer
Phone: +61 2 61316131
Email: foi@afp.gov.au

Australia Government
Office of the Australian Information Commissioner
Phone: +61 2 9284 9666
Email: enquiries@oaic.gov.au

Individuals may request correction to personal information pursuant to Commonwealth law, regulations and guidelines.

The Australian Federal Police
Freedom of Information contact officer
Phone: +61 2 61316131
Email: foi@afp.gov.au

Australia Government
Office of the Australian Information Commissioner
Phone: +61 2 9284 9666
Email: enquiries@oaic.gov.au

Appendix: N

Organizations:

The Governments of United States of America and the Republic of Austria

Purpose and Use:

The purpose of the Preventing and Combating Serious Crime (PCSC) agreements is to enhance and expedite cooperation between the Parties in preventing and combating serious crime. The PCSC agreements are designed to facilitate the timely exchange of case specific information between the signatories regarding the prevention, detection, and investigation of serious criminal activities. Serious criminal activity excludes minor criminal offenses and generally may have the effect of rendering an individual inadmissible or removable from the United States. This includes inquiries at the border when an individual has been identified for further inspection.

PCSC agreements do not provide for bulk screening or bulk sharing of data. The Agreements enable the parties' national contact points to query individual fingerprint records through an automated system. In individual cases where there is a match and in compliance with the supplying country's national law, the supplying country may supply the requesting country further information to assist with law enforcement efforts in both countries. In certain cases, for example terrorism related cases, with the foreign partner's permission data may be enrolled in IDENT. The PCSC agreement can facilitate near real-time law enforcement-to-law enforcement cooperation critical to the prevention and investigation of serious crime.

Individuals Impacted:

Information will be shared on individuals that are suspected or convicted of committing serious crimes. In addition to third party nationals, this can include citizens of both the United States and the Republic of Austria.

Data Elements:

Biometric data: digital facial photograph and fingerprints.

Biographic data: Data exchanged under this project may include (but not limited to): Name (first and last, other), Date fingerprinted, Reason fingerprinted, Location fingerprinted, Aliases, Nationality, Place of Birth, Date of Birth, Gender, Travel and Identity document information, Encounter information (Transaction-identifier data includes the sending organization; timestamp; reason sent, such as entry, visa application, credentialing application, or apprehension; and any available encounter information).

In the event of an information match, the partners may further collaborate and review the match by exchanging additional information allowable under applicable law to determine whether further action is required using other existing protocols (law enforcement or otherwise) between the countries.

Applicable IDENT SORN Routine Uses:

This sharing of information from IDENT on matches on biometric queries from the Republic of Austria is authorized by Routine Use "A" of the IDENT SORN, which states that records may be

disclosed to appropriate federal, state, local, tribal, foreign, or international agencies seeking information on the subjects of wants, warrants, or lookouts, or any other subject of interest for the specific purposes of administering or enforcing the law, national security, immigration, or intelligence, or carrying out DHS mission-related functions.

For queries going out from DHS, this sharing is authorized by DHS/ICE-011 - Immigration Enforcement Operational Records System (ENFORCE) May 3, 2010, 75 FR 23274.

Partner Notice:

The Republic of Austria does not provide public notice. Individuals have the right to access their personal information, but personal data is not available to the general public, pursuant to Article 26 Data Protection Law of 2000. Requests must be made to the ordering party (owner) of the collected data (public authorities or companies) in written form. Requests on personal data in the Central Criminal Data Register must be made to the relevant police authority.

Retention by Partner:

If there is no match to the initial query, all transmitted biometric information is deleted. The receiving country is required to destroy the biometric information in a secure manner and use it for no other purpose once the search against its relevant biometric systems is complete. If there is a match in the receiving country's database, the supplying country will determine whether or not sharing further information on the subject is permissible under its national law. When there is a legitimate purpose connected with a match, either country may store, process, and transmit biometric and biographical information shared through a follow-up exchange, in accordance with applicable national laws and established information retention policies.

Compliance Reporting:

Under the Agreement, the Parties are required to maintain documentation, such as audit logs of the transmission and receipt of data communicated under the Agreement. This documentation, and the systems which collect and store the subject data, will be periodically evaluated to ensure compliance with the terms set forth in the Agreement, applicable Interface Control Documents, and any other implementing arrangements. The Parties have agreed to cooperate with each other on requests for such documentation records.

Onward Transfer:

The PCSC agreement does not permit the further communication of data provided under the Agreement to any third State, international body, or private entity without the consent of the country that provided the data and without the appropriate safeguards.

Training:

Provides basic training to authorized system users.

Correction and Redress:

Individuals have the right to access their personal information, but personal data is not available to the general public, pursuant to Article 26 Data Protection Law of 2000. Requests must be made to the ordering party (owner) of the collected data (public authorities or companies) in written form. Requests on personal data in the Central Criminal Data Register must be made to the relevant police authority.

Individuals may request access to personal information to all public and private holders of their personal data, pursuant to the Austrian Data Protection Act from 2000. In case of doubt on who is in charge of the data or for general information the Point of Contact is:

Austria Data Protection Commission (Datenschutzkommission)
Hohenstaufengasse 3
A-1010 Vienna
Phone: +43 1 531 15-202525
Fax: +43 1 531 15-202690
Email: dsk@dsk.gv.at

Individuals may request correction to (or deletion of) personal information pursuant to Article 27 of the Data Protection Law of 2000 to the holders of their personal data. If the request is not accepted, the individual can lodge a complaint to the:

Austria Data Protection Commission (Datenschutzkommission)
Hohenstaufengasse 3
A-1010 Vienna
Phone: +43 1 531 15-202525
Fax: +43 1 531 15-202690
Email: dsk@dsk.gv.at

Appendix: O

Organizations:

The Governments of United States of America and the Kingdom of Denmark

Purpose and Use:

The purpose of the Preventing and Combating Serious Crime (PCSC) agreements is to enhance and expedite cooperation between the Parties in preventing and combating serious crime. The PCSC agreements are designed to facilitate the timely exchange of case specific information between the signatories regarding the prevention, detection, and investigation of serious criminal activities. Serious criminal activity excludes minor criminal offenses and generally may have the effect of rendering an individual inadmissible or removable from the United States. This includes inquiries at the border when an individual has been identified for further inspection.

PCSC agreements do not provide for bulk screening or bulk sharing of data. The Agreements enable the parties' national contact points to query individual fingerprint records through an automated system. In individual cases where there is a match and in compliance with the supplying country's national law, the supplying country may supply the requesting country further information to assist with law enforcement efforts in both countries. In certain cases, for example terrorism related cases, with the foreign partner's permission data may be enrolled in IDENT. The PCSC agreement can facilitate near real-time law enforcement-to-law enforcement cooperation critical to the prevention and investigation of serious crime.

Individuals Impacted:

Information will be shared on individuals that are suspected or convicted of committing serious crimes. In addition to third party nationals, this can include citizens of both the United States and the Kingdom of Denmark.

Data Elements:

Biometric data: digital facial photograph and fingerprints

Biographic data: Data exchanged under this project may include (but not limited to):

Name (first and last, other), Date fingerprinted, Reason fingerprinted, Location fingerprinted, Aliases, Nationality, Place of Birth, Date of Birth, Gender, Travel and Identity document information, Encounter information (Transaction-identifier data includes the sending organization; timestamp; reason sent, such as entry, visa application, credentialing application, or apprehension; and any available encounter information).

In the event of an information match, the partners may further collaborate and review the match by exchanging additional information allowable under applicable law to determine whether further action is required using other existing protocols (law enforcement or otherwise) between the countries.

Applicable IDENT SORN Routine Uses:

This sharing of information from IDENT on matches on biometric queries from the Kingdom of Denmark is authorized by Routine Use "A" of the IDENT SORN, which states that records may be disclosed to appropriate federal, state, local, tribal, foreign, or international agencies seeking information on the subjects of wants, warrants, or lookouts, or any other subject of interest for the specific purposes of administering or enforcing the law, national security, immigration, or intelligence, or carrying out DHS mission-related functions.

For queries going out from DHS, this sharing is authorized by DHS/ICE-011 - Immigration Enforcement Operational Records System (ENFORCE) May 3, 2010, 75 FR 23274.

Partner Notice:

The Kingdom of Denmark provides public notice on the collection of personal information through the public website for the Danish Police (www.politi.dk) and the official website for the Danish Data Protection Agency (www.datatilsynet.dk).

Retention by Partner:

If there is no match to the initial query, all transmitted biometric information is deleted. The receiving country is required to destroy the biometric information in a secure manner and use it for no other purpose once the search against its relevant biometric systems is complete. If there is a match in the receiving country's database, the supplying country will determine whether or not sharing further information on the subject is permissible under its national law. When there is a legitimate purpose connected with a match, either country may store, process, and transmit biometric and biographical information shared through a follow-up exchange, in accordance with applicable national laws and established information retention policies.

Compliance Reporting:

Under the Agreement, the Parties are required to maintain documentation, such as audit logs of the transmission and receipt of data communicated under the Agreement. This documentation, and the systems which collect and store the subject data, will be periodically evaluated to ensure compliance with the terms set forth in the Agreement, applicable Interface Control Documents, and any other implementing arrangements. The Parties have agreed to cooperate with each other on requests for such documentation records.

Onward Transfer:

The PCSC agreement does not permit the further communication of data provided under the Agreement to any third State, international body, or private entity without the consent of the country that provided the data and without the appropriate safeguards.

Training:

The Kingdom of Denmark provides basic training for all system users and also a follow up training as ongoing training needs and changes in legislation dictate.

Correction and Redress:

Access: Individuals may request access to personal information through the local police district or through the Danish National Police. Information requests can be filed by mail or email. Contact information is available through the official website for the Danish Police (www.politi.dk).

Redress: Individuals may request correction to personal information pursuant to legislation, regulations and guidelines through the local police district or through the Danish National Police. Requests can be filed by mail or email. Contact information is available through the official website for the Danish Police (www.politi.dk).

In addition, individuals may file a complaint with the Danish Data Protection Agency on whether personal data has been processed in accordance with the Danish Act on Processing of Personal Data (www.datatilsynet.dk).

Appendix: P

Organizations:

The Governments of United States of America and the Republic of Finland

Purpose and Use:

The purpose of the Preventing and Combating Serious Crime (PCSC) agreements is to enhance and expedite cooperation between the Parties in preventing and combating serious crime. The PCSC agreements are designed to facilitate the timely exchange of case specific information between the signatories regarding the prevention, detection, and investigation of serious criminal activities. Serious criminal activity excludes minor criminal offenses and generally has the effect of rendering an individual inadmissible or removable from the United States. This includes inquiries at the border when an individual has been identified for further inspection.

PCSC agreements do not provide for bulk screening or bulk sharing of data. The Agreements enable the parties' national contact points to query individual fingerprint records through an automated system. In individual cases where there is a match and in compliance with the supplying country's national law, the supplying country may supply the requesting country further information to assist with law enforcement efforts in both countries. The PCSC agreement can facilitate near real-time law enforcement-to-law enforcement cooperation critical to the prevention and investigation of serious crime.

Individuals Impacted:

Information will be shared on individuals that are suspected or convicted of committing serious crimes. In addition to third party nationals, this can include citizens of both the United States and the Republic of Finland.

Data Elements:

Biometric data: digital facial photograph and fingerprints

Biographic data: Data exchanged under this project may include (but not limited to):

Name (first and last, other), Date fingerprinted, Reason fingerprinted, Location fingerprinted, Aliases, Nationality, Place of Birth, Date of Birth, Gender, Travel and Identity document information, Encounter information (Transaction-identifier data includes the sending organization; timestamp; reason sent, such as entry, visa application, credentialing application, or apprehension; and any available encounter information).

In the event of an information match, the partners may further collaborate and review the match by exchanging additional information allowable under applicable law to determine whether further action is required using other existing protocols (law enforcement or otherwise) between the countries.

Applicable IDENT SORN Routine Uses:

This sharing of information from IDENT on matches on biometric queries from the Republic of Finland is authorized by Routine Use "A" of the IDENT SORN, which states that records may be

disclosed to appropriate federal, state, local, tribal, foreign, or international agencies seeking information on the subjects of wants, warrants, or lookouts, or any other subject of interest for the specific purposes of administering or enforcing the law, national security, immigration, or intelligence, or carrying out DHS mission-related functions.

For queries going out from DHS, this sharing is authorized by DHS/ICE-011 - Immigration Enforcement Operational Records System (ENFORCE) May 3, 2010, 75 FR 23274.

Partner Notice:

The Republic of Finland provides public notice of how personal information is collected and handled through different registers in various acts, but especially in the Personal Data Act (523/1999). Other relevant legislation giving notice to individuals are the Act on the Processing of Personal Data by the Police (761/2003), the Act on the Protection of Privacy in Working Life (759/2004) as well as the Act on the Protection of Privacy in Electronic Communications (516/2004). When data is given from a register belonging to a public authority, the Act on the Openness of Government Activities (621/1999) applies.

All the legal acts related to the handling of personal data can be found on the public website for legal acts (www.finlex.fi). Additionally, information on the handling of personal data can be found on the websites of the Data Protection Ombudsman (www.tietosuoja.fi).

Retention by Partner:

If there is no match to the initial query, all transmitted biometric information is deleted. The receiving country is required to destroy the biometric information in a secure manner and use it for no other purpose once the search against its relevant biometric systems is complete. If there is a match in the receiving country's database, the supplying country will determine whether or not sharing further information on the subject is permissible under its national law. When there is a legitimate purpose connected with a match, either country may store, process, and transmit biometric and biographical information shared through a follow-up exchange, in accordance with applicable national laws and established information retention policies.

Compliance Reporting:

Under the Agreement, the Parties are required to maintain documentation, such as audit logs of the transmission and receipt of data communicated under the Agreement. This documentation, and the systems which collect and store the subject data, will be periodically evaluated to ensure compliance with the terms set forth in the Agreement, applicable Interface Control Documents, and any other implementing arrangements. The Parties have agreed to cooperate with each other on requests for such documentation records.

Onward Transfer:

The PCSC agreement does not permit the further communication of data provided under the Agreement to any third State, international body, or private entity without the consent of the country that provided the data and without the appropriate safeguards.

Training:

There is no specific clause in the Finnish legislation regarding training on processing of data, but the legislation implies that the personnel in charge of the processing of the data is adequately trained for the purpose. The Data Protection Ombudsman and the Office of the Data Protection Ombudsman provide guidance and advice on the processing of personal data, organize trainings on demand and control the observance of the law.

Correction and Redress:

When a data subject wants to use one of the rights granted by the Personal Data Act (right of information on the processing of data; right of access, rectification, right to prohibit processing) or when the data subject has a query about the handling of his/her data, they should first contact the controller in charge of processing the data. If the matter cannot be dealt with the controller, the data subject can contact the Data Protection Ombudsman. If the processing of the data seems unlawful, the data subject can ask the Police to investigate the matter.

Office of the Data Protection Ombudsman
P.O. Box 315
FIN-00181 HELSINKI
FINLAND

Address:
Albertinkatu 25 A, 3rd floor
E-mail: tietosuoja@om.fi

Tel: +358 29 56 66700 (exchange)

Appendix: Q

Organizations:

The Governments of United States of America and the Federal Republic of Germany

Purpose and Use:

The purpose of the Preventing and Combating Serious Crime (PCSC) agreements is to enhance and expedite cooperation between the Parties in preventing and combating serious crime. The PCSC agreements are designed to facilitate the timely exchange of case specific information between the signatories regarding the prevention, detection, and investigation of serious criminal activities. Serious criminal activity excludes minor criminal offenses and generally has the effect of rendering an individual inadmissible or removable from the United States. This includes inquiries at the border when an individual has been identified for further inspection.

PCSC agreements do not provide for bulk screening or bulk sharing of data. The Agreements enable the parties' national contact points to query individual fingerprint records through an automated system. In individual cases where there is a match and in compliance with the supplying country's national law, the supplying country may supply the requesting country further information to assist with law enforcement efforts in both countries. The PCSC agreement can facilitate near real-time law enforcement-to-law enforcement cooperation critical to the prevention and investigation of serious crime.

Individuals Impacted:

Information will be shared on individuals that are suspected or convicted of committing serious crimes. In addition to third party nationals, this can include citizens of both the United States and the Federal Republic of Germany.

Data Elements:

Biometric data: digital facial photograph and fingerprints

Biographic data: Data exchanged under this project may include (but not limited to):

Name (first and last, other), Date fingerprinted, Reason fingerprinted, Location fingerprinted, Aliases, Nationality, Place of Birth, Date of Birth, Gender, Travel and Identity document information, Encounter information (Transaction-identifier data includes the sending organization; timestamp; reason sent, such as entry, visa application, credentialing application, or apprehension; and any available encounter information).

In the event of an information match, the partners may further collaborate and review the match by exchanging additional information allowable under applicable law to determine whether further action is required using other existing protocols (law enforcement or otherwise) between the countries.

Applicable IDENT SORN Routine Uses:

This sharing of information from IDENT on matches on biometric queries from the Federal Republic of Germany is authorized by Routine Use "A" of the IDENT SORN, which states that records may be disclosed to appropriate federal, state, local, tribal, foreign, or international agencies seeking information on the subjects of wants, warrants, or lookouts, or any other subject of interest for the specific purposes of administering or enforcing the law, national security, immigration, or intelligence, or carrying out DHS mission-related functions.

For queries going out from DHS, this sharing is authorized by DHS/ICE-011 - Immigration Enforcement Operational Records System (ENFORCE) May 3, 2010, 75 FR 23274.

Partner Notice:

In Germany, the relevant information on notifications can be found directly in the specific laws regulating the respective data processing. These laws include – similar to the "Systems of Record Notices" – information on the purpose of processing data and rights of individuals (such as transmission/retention of data) and duties (such as deletion) of the respective agency processing the data. Relevant legal bases include the Federal Data Protection Act (BDSG) that contains general requirements (e.g. section 12 et seq) and in the case of PCSC, the Federal Criminal Police Office Act (Bundeskriminalamtgesetz- BKAG) (e.g. section 7 et seq) as *lex specialis*.

Retention by Partner:

If there is no match to the initial query, all transmitted biometric information is deleted. The receiving country is required to destroy the biometric information in a secure manner and use it for no other purpose once the search against its relevant biometric systems is complete. If there is a match in the receiving country's database, the supplying country will determine whether or not sharing further information on the subject is permissible under its national law. When there is a legitimate purpose connected with a match, either country may store, process, and transmit biometric and biographical information shared through a follow-up exchange, in accordance with applicable national laws and established information retention policies.

Compliance Reporting:

Under the Agreement, the Parties are required to maintain documentation, such as audit logs of the transmission and receipt of data communicated under the Agreement. This documentation, and the systems which collect and store the subject data, will be periodically evaluated to ensure compliance with the terms set forth in the Agreement, applicable Interface Control Documents, and any other implementing arrangements. The Parties have agreed to cooperate with each other on requests for such documentation records.

Onward Transfer:

The PCSC agreement does not permit the further communication of data provided under the Agreement to any third State, international body, or private entity without the consent of the country that provided the data and without the appropriate safeguards.

Training:

All public service employees who work with personal data are trained accordingly. Data protection officers of government agencies are required by law to provide advising and training.

Correction and Redress:

Under Section 19 of the Federal Data Protection Act (Bundesdatenschutzgesetz, BDSG) in conjunction with Section 12 (5) of the Federal Criminal Police Office Act (Bundeskriminalamtgesetz, BKAG), individuals may request information about their personal data on file. If a request is refused, individuals may have recourse to the administrative courts. Individuals may also request the assistance of the Federal Commissioner for Data Protection and Freedom of Information.

For access to information held on them, individuals may reach out to:

Bundeskriminalamt (Federal Criminal Police Office)
Der Datenschutzbeauftragte (Data protection officer)
65173 Wiesbaden
dsrecht@bka.bund.de

For correction and redress:

Bundesministerium des Innern (Federal Ministry of the Interior)
Arbeitsgruppe ÖS I 3 (Task Force ÖS I 3)
Alt-Moabit 101 D
10559 Berlin
OESI3AG@bmi.bund.de

Appendix: R

Organizations:

The Governments of United States of America and Taiwan

Purpose and Use:

The purpose of the Preventing and Combating Serious Crime (PCSC) agreements is to enhance and expedite cooperation between the Parties in preventing and combating serious crime. The PCSC agreements are designed to facilitate the timely exchange of case specific information between the signatories regarding the prevention, detection, and investigation of serious criminal activities. Serious criminal activity excludes minor criminal offenses and generally may have the effect of rendering an individual inadmissible or removable from the United States. This includes inquiries at the border when an individual has been identified for further inspection.

PCSC agreements do not provide for bulk screening or bulk sharing of data. The Agreements enable the parties' national contact points to query individual fingerprint records through an automated system. In individual cases where there is a match and in compliance with the supplying country's national law, the supplying country may supply the requesting country further information to assist with law enforcement efforts in both countries. In certain cases, for example terrorism related cases, with the foreign partner's permission data may be enrolled in IDENT. The PCSC agreement can facilitate near real-time law enforcement-to-law enforcement cooperation critical to the prevention and investigation of serious crime.

Individuals Impacted:

Information will be shared on individuals that are suspected or convicted of committing serious crimes. In addition to third party nationals, this can include citizens of both the United States and Taiwan.

Data Elements:

Biometric data: digital facial photograph and fingerprints

Biographic data: Data exchanged under this project may include (but not limited to):

Name (first and last, other), Date fingerprinted, Reason fingerprinted, Location fingerprinted, Aliases, Nationality, Place of Birth, Date of Birth, Gender, Travel and Identity document information, Encounter information (Transaction-identifier data includes the sending organization; timestamp; reason sent, such as entry, visa application, credentialing application, or apprehension; and any available encounter information).

In the event of an information match, the partners may further collaborate and review the match by exchanging additional information allowable under applicable law to determine whether further action is required using other existing protocols (law enforcement or otherwise) between the countries.

Applicable IDENT SORN Routine Uses:

This sharing of information from IDENT on matches on biometric queries from Taiwan is authorized by Routine Use "A" of the IDENT SORN, which states that records may be disclosed to appropriate federal, state, local, tribal, foreign, or international agencies seeking information on the subjects of wants, warrants, or lookouts, or any other subject of interest for the specific purposes of administering or enforcing the law, national security, immigration, or intelligence, or carrying out DHS mission-related functions.

For queries going out from DHS, this sharing is authorized by DHS/ICE-011 - Immigration Enforcement Operational Records System (ENFORCE) May 3, 2010, 75 FR 23274.

Partner Notice:

Notifications of collections of personal information are in accordance with Articles 8, 15, and 19 of the Personal Information Protection Act (PIPA) and notifications of usage of personal information are in accordance with Articles 9, 15, and 19 of the PIPA

Retention by Partner:

If there is no match to the initial query, all transmitted biometric information is deleted. The receiving country is required to destroy the biometric information in a secure manner and use it for no other purpose once the search against its relevant biometric systems is complete. If there is a match in the receiving country's database, the supplying country will determine whether or not sharing further information on the subject is permissible under its national law. When there is a legitimate purpose connected with a match, either country may store, process, and transmit biometric and biographical information shared through a follow-up exchange, in accordance with applicable national laws and established information retention policies.

Compliance Reporting:

Under the Agreement, the Parties are required to maintain documentation, such as audit logs of the transmission and receipt of data communicated under the Agreement. This documentation, and the systems which collect and store the subject data, will be periodically evaluated to ensure compliance with the terms set forth in the Agreement, applicable Interface Control Documents, and any other implementing arrangements. The Parties have agreed to cooperate with each other on requests for such documentation records.

Onward Transfer:

The PCSC agreement does not permit the further communication of data provided under the Agreement to any third State, international body, or private entity without the consent of the country that provided the data and without the appropriate safeguards.

Training:

Training is provided to all authorized users.

Correction and Redress:

International Criminal Affairs Division of

National Police Agency's Criminal Investigation Bureau

Republic of China (Taiwan)

Email: CIBPCSC@email.cib.gov.tw

Telephone: +886 2 27697390

Redress:

International Criminal Affairs Division of

 National Police Agency's Criminal Investigation Bureau

Republic of China (Taiwan)

Email: CIBPCSC@email.cib.gov.tw

Telephone: +886 2 27697390

(Forensic Biology Office, Fingerprint Office, Criminal Records Section

Criminal Intelligence Office

Internal Affairs Office of National Police Agency's Criminal Investigation Bureau

Republic of China (Taiwan))